THE
ENCYCLOPAEDIA
OF
FLOWER
ARRANGING
TECHNIQUES

THE
ENCYCLOPAEDIA
OF
FLOWER
ARRANGING
TECHNIQUES

MARCIA HURST

A QUARTO BOOK

This edition published in 2003 by
Apple Press
Sheridan House
112-116 A Western Road
Hove
East Sussex
www.apple-press.com

Reprinted 2004

Copyright © 1996, 2003 Quarto Publishing plc

This book was designed and produced by
Quarto Publishing
The Old Brewery
6 Blundell Street
London N7 9BH

ISBN 1 84092 423 3

QUAR.EFT

Senior editor Sally MacEachern
Editor Judith Casey
Senior art editor Liz Brown
Designer Sheila Volpe
Photographers Paul Forrester, Laura Wickenden,
Colin Bowling
Picture researcher Susannah Jayes
Picture research manager Guilia Hetherington
Editorial director Mark Dartford
Art director Moira Clinch

Typeset by Central Southern Typesetters, Eastbourne
Manufactured in Singapore by Bright Arts, (Singapore)
Pte Ltd
Printed in China by SNP Leefung Printers
Ltd

CONTENTS

INTRODUCTION

Have you ever admired a beautiful flower

arrangement and wondered how it was achieved? If

you enjoy arranging flowers in a vase and would like

to try some more ambitious designs, then you need

to learn some of the florist's secrets.

Of course, part of the art of the professional florist is to conceal the tools of the trade: florist's foam holds the flowers at the right angle and at the right spacing and is concealed with plenty of foliage; flowers with soft stems are wired to enable you to bend and shape them.

From tips on conditioning flowers to make them last longer, to positioning the last flower in an elaborate arrangement, there are a whole wealth of techniques to learn. This book will show you how to get the most from fresh and dried flowers to create original and attractive arrangements.

▲ **Pew end**
This pew end arrangement is made on a spray tray which holds a quarter block of soaking wet foam. You need florist's tape to fix the foam on the tray and to attach the tray to the wood.

▶ **Dried flower basket**
The dried flower basket is packed with foam specially formulated for dried and artificial flowers. It is a grey polyurethane foam, which holds the stems much more firmly than the soaking type.

TOOLS AND MATERIALS

For any new skill there is always a list of recommended tools and materials. The selection shown here will prepare you for any of the arrangements in this book. The list may seem daunting but not all the items are expensive and you can build up your tool kit gradually.

Many of the materials and equipment used in flower arranging and floristry are specialised and they are generally only available from some flower shops and garden centres. If you use your local flower shop regularly and find them helpful, you should be able to buy or order the materials from them. Alternatively, if you take part in classes or belong to a floral arts group, then you will be able to obtain most things through the instructor. Floristry sundry wholesalers supply the trade with all these products, but they usually have a minimum purchase requirement.

1 | Florist's foam for fresh flowers

Green foam blocks generally known by the brand name of "Oasis", are designed to quickly soak up water (within 90 seconds). It is very versatile and can be cut to shape and packed in to a container, making a firm base for arranging flowers. Foam is also available in a small cylinder shape.

2 | Plastic dishes for foam

These come in three sizes and are available in white or green (green is less conspicuous). The design shown here has an oblong base, which takes either a quarter or a third cut from a block of foam.

3 | Candle holder

The pointed end is designed to push down firmly in to foam. It will take a standard size candle.

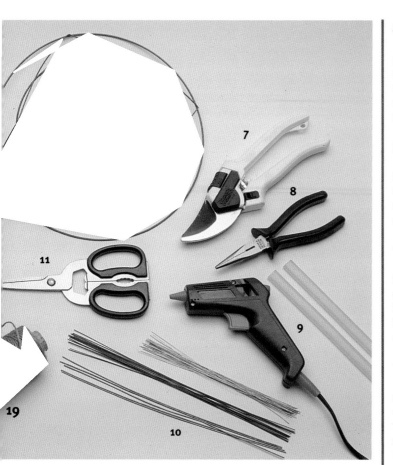

8 | Pliers
You may prefer to use pliers with a wire cutting section in the middle for cutting through wire instead of using scissors. Not an essential tool.

9 | Glue gun and sticks
An indispensable tool which is particularly useful for creating some of the more ambitious pieces such as the wreaths and pictures.

10 | Florist's wire
This comes in various thicknesses and lengths according to requirements and is measured both in metric and imperial gauges (see section on Wires and Wiring).

11 | Scissors
These are strong, sharp specialist scissors, sharp enough to cut cleanly through tough stems. Household scissors with long blades are not suitable.

12 | Flower food
A specially developed product, formulated to extend vase life by feeding the flowers and inhibiting the growth of bacteria in the water.

13 | Silver wire
Also known as rose wire, it is used where delicacy and lightness is required (see section on Wires and Wiring) and is available in two grades.

14 | Florist's pot tape
Available in dark green or white and in two widths, it is used to anchor the florist's foam securely to the container.

15 | Florist's stem tape
There are three types of tape: a slightly sticky crepe-like tape with the brand name of Stemtex; the original stem tape known as Guttacoll; and stretchy self-sealing tape called Parafilm. Try out the different types to see which suits your purposes (see section on Wires and Wiring).

16 | Spray tray
This green plastic container was originally designed for making funeral sprays but it is ideal for making the pew end arrangements for a wedding.

17 | Dry foam
This grey foam is the non-soaking variety formulated for arranging dried and artificial flowers.

18 | Chicken wire
This is standard width chicken wire available from most hardware and DIY stores and has a variety of uses (see sections on Topiary and Containers).

19 | Garden twine
Used to hand-tie bouquets.

20 | Pins
Used to attach buttonholes to lapels.

4 | Candle cup
This chrome-plated plastic bowl takes half a cylinder of foam and is designed to sit in the middle branch of a formal candelabra in place of a candle. Unscrew the section that holds the candle to make space for the cup with its decoration.

5 | Wire wreath frame
Copper wire rings come in increasing diameters from 26cm (10in) upwards. Extra large ones can be made to order.

6 | Wire-edged ribbon
A ribbon with a fine wire incorporated in to each edge, which makes bow making with flimsy fabric much easier. This ribbon is available from some stationers as well as florists shops.

7 | Secateurs
Available from all garden centres and hardware stores, they are useful for tough stems of greenery.

TOOLS AND MATERIALS

The easiest way to explain how to use a tool or a floristry material is to see it in action. Throughout this book there are step-by-step photographs illustrating how many of the floristry techniques are achieved. Some of them will need some practice, such as stretching stem tape as you bind the stems together, while other techniques can be picked up straight away. Here are some of the basic techniques that appear in the arrangements.

▲ **Hot glue gun**

These guns have made it possible to make creative pieces simply and quickly. The hot glue cools down rapidly and makes a strong bond immediately. There are guns available now that heat glue at a lower temperature as scorched finger tips can be a problem if you aren't careful.

▲ **Rustic basket prepared with chicken wire**

If your basket is already lined with a good plastic lining, you can simply pack it with scrunched up chicken wire. If the lining seems likely to perforate, it's best to double line it with some bin liner as a precaution. Chicken wire is excellent for use with spring flowers, instead of foam.

▲ **Garden twine**

Ordinary lightweight garden twine is ideal for tying off the stems of hand-tied bunches. It is strong enough to hold without damaging even the most delicate stems. Either green or natural is suitable.

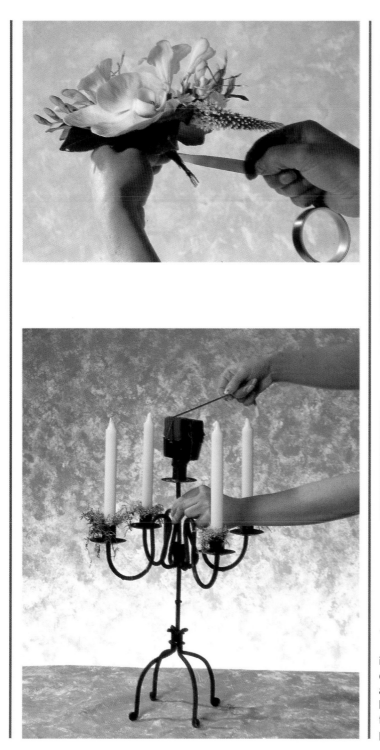

◀ Stem tape

This is the stretchable type of tape being used here to finish off a hat decoration. Stretch the end of the tape until it is almost transparent, then bind it on to the stem, stretching the tape as you work to make a lightweight finish, and giving it a final stretch to seal.

▲ Chicken wire stretched over a form

Chicken wire can be used to make a shape and to hold foam in place.

◀ Candle cup

Candle cups are available in chrome to fit in silver candelabras, or in black to suit an iron candelabra as shown here. The whole container is firmly taped in position with pot tape.

TECHNIQUES

It is possible to make beautiful flower arrangements without any technical knowledge. However, familiarity with basic techniques such as colour, design and wiring will give you confidence and help you to explore your creativity. If you want to enter competitions or arrange flowers professionally, understanding some of the basic rules of flower arranging is essential.

ACCESSORIES

Flowers can form an essential component of a

carefully planned display, for instance on a

mantelpiece or a side table, placed

among a collection of well-loved

ornaments and framed family

photographs. Open any

interior design magazine these

days and you will see that no

setting is complete without a

well-thought-out selection of fresh or

dried flowers arranged informally to enhance the

whole decorative scheme.

To achieve a well balanced effect, pick a container that will complement the other accessories in the setting. Choose your flowers with the colour scheme in mind, perhaps taking a piece of fabric and the container with you to help with your selection. As the flowers are there to enhance rather than dominate, a simple arrangement of two or three varieties with a little foliage will be more effective than an elaborate display.

> **FURTHER INFORMATION**
> ☞
> Containers, page **38**

KITCHEN SCALES ARRANGEMENT

This dainty summer arrangement would look enchanting on the shelves of an old dresser or on a pine kitchen table, grouped with other attractive pieces of "kitchenalia".

1 Tape florist's foam on to the plate that usually takes the weights. You will only need a small square as the finished arrangement won't be very large; it is a good idea to trim the foam to create a more compact shape.

2 Use the foliage to create the overall shape, making sure to cut the stems quite short and to cover the foam.

3 | Marguerites are simple and charming daisies, just right for the informality of this piece. Push them into the foam, level with the foliage.

4 | Bright red anemones continue the informal theme. Anemones are not always easy to push into the foam, so try to use them early on in the process before the foam is filled with too many stems.

5 | Creamy white roses add a touch of luxury to the piece. If you are doing this arrangement in the summer, why not use some of your garden roses instead of florist's roses. They may not be as perfect but they open beautifully and are usually delightfully scented. If you have any jasmine growing in your garden, a few pieces trailing over the edge look pretty and smell wonderful.

6 | To balance the scales and complement the summer arrangement, empty a punnet of luscious strawberries on to the other plate.

ARTIFICIAL FLOWERS

Silk flowers are perfect for creating a display in a permanent setting, such as a hall or reception area, where fresh flowers would be too expensive or impractical.

Although very few artificial flowers are made of silk these days, the term is still generally used.

Most artificial flowers are made from polyester, with coated wire for support and to allow for a natural bend in stems and leaves. In most cases the flowers are designed to be as realistic as possible, and this realism can be enhanced by arranging the flowers as informally and naturally as possible, combining them with good quality foliage.

As the initial outlay will be quite pricey, selecting suitable material is essential. The range of material available these days is almost overwhelming, but you can narrow your choice by selecting blooms based on the colour scheme of your room, that have year-round interest, that suit the position in the room in terms of scale, and that have the right touch of formality or informality.

WEDDING FLOWERS Silk flowers are also extremely popular for bridal work and for hat decoration. They have the great advantage of being ready well in advance of the event, with no danger of wilting blooms! Delicate blooms can be cut up into small clusters and wired on to an alice band or wire frame to make lovely hair pieces, following the same principles shown in the sections on wiring. Larger flowers are effective on a hat with a large brim; build up a design on to a wire base and then stitch in place.

> **FURTHER INFORMATION**
> ☞
> Wiring, page **114**
> Hat decoration, page **84**

JUG ARRANGEMENT

The container for this piece is an extremely bright Italian hand-painted jug with lots of clashing colours. Somehow all these bright Mediterranean colours seem to work together very well; perhaps the blue has a cooling effect on the more vivid oranges. As the jug itself is making a strong statement, it is important to choose colours and shapes that are robust enough not to be dominated by the container.

1 Prepare the jug with dry florist's foam and start arranging the stems of orange flowers in a gentle fan shape to the finished height.

2 These lovely shiny black berries make an attractive contrast in form and texture with flowers and add depth to the arrangement. Artificial fruit and berries are being used much more in silk flower arrangements and there is now a wide choice available. Arrange the stems to follow the general fan shape of the orange flowers.

7 ▎ Ivy always adds a gentle touch of informality to any piece, be it fresh or artificial, and in this case, it makes a perfect counter-balance to the jug handle.

3 ▎ Some silk flowers carry several blooms which can be broken down into smaller sections. It can be difficult to cut through the wire stems with scissors, so you may need wire cutters as well.

5 ▎ Arrange the purple-blue aster-type flowers following the general fan shape of the orange flowers.

4 ▎ The blue bell-shaped flowers are the focal point to the piece, so arrange them deep in the centre of the arrangement.

6 ▎ Add some interesting foliage stems like these maple leaves to create movement in the design. Their beautiful flame colours will enhance the autumnal effect. You will probably find it is best to break the stems down into smaller pieces.

BASKETS AND BOXES

Most flowers are arranged in vases or jugs, but it is fun to vary the container, particularly if you enjoy arranging dried flowers. Old and new baskets make delightful containers and they also make wonderful gifts when filled with fresh or dried flowers.

However, for something a little different, why not go rummaging through your local junk shop to see what you can find? All sorts of unlikely containers can be pressed into service and can provide great inspiration. For instance, solid old tool boxes, cutlery trays, and Victorian and Edwardian biscuit tins with hinged lids and lovely faded patterns make interesting choices. Modern baskets come in a great variety of shapes and forms often with a textured finish such as moss and fern. Some have a rustic effect achieved by leaving the bark on the weaving material. A good selection of modern boxes and trays made from recycled wood can also be found in flower and gift shops; these make excellent containers. As with vases and jugs, it would be worth building up a collection, which would also look decorative in your home even when unfilled.

DRIED ARRANGEMENT IN A WORKBOX

This chunky old workbox, found in a junk shop, makes a wonderful container for dried flowers. The box is divided into compartments which can be filled with different things such as a bunch of dried lavender and loose lavender. Keep your eyes open for old boxes like this as they are always fun to use.

1 Fill one compartment with a bag of dried lavender.

2 Pack two more compartments with florist's foam for dried flowers.

5 | Gradually build up your design with groups of flowers, keeping all the heads level. This selection includes dried lavender, wheat, poppyheads, dark blue larkspur and echinops as well as the helianthus.

3 | Pack some dry moss into the gaps between the box and the foam to secure it firmly in position.

4 | Arrange the flower stems in groups, starting with a bunch of small helianthus (a kind of sunflower).

6 | Arrange the remaining bunches so that they gently curve round towards the front of the box, at the same time decreasing in height. Pack more moss around the stems and on top of the foam.

7 For a final touch, place a large bunch of lavender tied with a piece of raffia in the front compartment.

▲ An unstripped willow basket filled with chicken wire, prepared for a fresh flower arrangement. Take care when using chicken wire (an old-fashioned but effective anchoring material) that the wire doesn't pierce the plastic liner of the basket. As a precaution, it may be worth double lining it with a piece of bin liner cut to size.

▶ A pretty basket with a handle, lined with bin liner and filled with florist's foam then packed with moss instead of securing it with florist's tape.

▲ An interesting selection of containers suitable for dried flower arrangements, including an old wooden cutlery tray, Victorian biscuit tins and a sweet Victorian egg basket, as well as modern rustic baskets.

BOUQUETS

The traditional presentation of a bouquet in a flat-backed case of paper and cellophane, is only one way of presenting flowers. In Holland a new technique of hand tying flowers has been developed so that when the gift wrapping is removed the flowers are ready to go straight in the vase with no further attention.

Using the technique of hand tying flowers, you can create beautiful arrangements for gifts and for special occasions such as weddings and christenings; you may also wish to make a tribute for a funeral.

CHOOSING FLOWERS The art of arranging flowers in a bouquet is the same as for all the other techniques shown in this book. The flowers should be selected for their colour, their shape and the lengths of their stem. You will also need a good selection of fresh foliage to enhance and fill out the flowers and to act as a base for the flower stems. To develop this skill, why not practise with flowers from your garden. To start with, disregard the colours and shapes, just concentrate on the technique of spiralling the stems.

FINISHING TOUCHES If you want to make a really impressive bunch as a gift then you will need cellophane and ribbon to give a professional finish, but a charming presentation can be made with tissue paper, white or coloured. Even brown paper can look stunning wrapped round a simple bunch of spring flowers.

> **FURTHER INFORMATION**
> 👉
> Wedding, page **106**

LARGE HAND-TIED BOUQUET

This is a big showy bouquet, suitable for any occasion that calls for a floral gesture. Once it is taken out of its wrapping, the bunch will balance beautifully in a large vase. All the recipient needs to do is to keep the vase topped up with water.

To make the following bouquet you will need: suitable foliage, 5 stems of aconitum, 3 stems of pink lily, 3 stems of antirrhinum, 3 stems of phlox, and a 60cm (24in) length of garden twine or raffia. Trim all the leaves off the flowers and foliage below what will eventually become the water line, approximately one-third of the overall height. The presentation is finished with cellophane, tissue paper and raffia.

1 As the finished piece is going to be tall and very full, you will need several good pieces of foliage. When placing foliage, select pieces that "grow" in the right direction. Starting with the foliage gives you a firm foundation in which to place the flower stems. If you make the bouquet without greenery, you will find the stems slide and twist out of control, and that the finished bunch looks gappy and lacking in depth. Greenery should never be considered as a filler. The colour green evokes freshness and tranquillity, and juxtaposed with the blooms intensifies their colours.

2 Place the tall, straight aconitum stems around your foliage foundation. With this technique, hold the stems in your left hand (reversed if you are left-handed) always using your right hand to place the flowers from top left to bottom right in a spiral. The stems will lie neatly and firmly in parallel lines in your left hand as you build up the bunch; you will also need to transfer the whole bunch from hand to hand to add some of the larger stems (see step 4 for more detail). The point where you hold the bunch should be roughly one-third of the overall height.

4 As the piece becomes larger, you will find it difficult to place the stems without moving the bunch. Transfer the whole bunch from left to right hand, then back again, but this time place the bunch back in the left hand with everything turned round by 45 degrees. This is how you place big blooms like these magnificent pink oriental lilies just where you want them to show to most advantage. When you have placed the first lily, you will have to continue turning the bouquet for each bloom.

3 Another tall strong flower, the antirrhinum, is added at this early stage to help in the development of the overall shape. Always remember to lay the stems as in step 1.

If you feel tempted to cross your stems, your finished piece will be too bulky with stems that crush against each other instead of lying parallel.

5 Following steps 3 and 4, continue adding the other blooms; the lilies, the rest of the antirrhinums and the delicately scented panicles of phlox. Position each bloom so that it can be clearly seen and is not crowded by other blooms or foliage. Take your time arranging each bloom, as once in position it will not be easy to remove.

6 With all the flowers assembled to your satisfaction, you need to secure them. With your right hand, pick up your piece of twine or raffia, and wind it round the stems immediately above your left hand, making sure that you have left a loose piece of about 20cm (8in) for the final tying process. With all the stems placed correctly in a spiral, you can pull the twine quite tightly at this binding point, without damaging even delicate stems.

8 Taking two pieces of tissue paper, fold each one over to form two triangles. Use each piece to cover the binding point of the stems with the triangles pointing up, slightly overlapping the two pieces. Give the paper a firm "scrunch" to hold it in place.

7 After you have secured the twine with a final knot, cut off all the stems to the same length. The whole piece should be perfectly balanced.

9 Cut two pieces of cellophane into squares slightly larger than the tissue, and folding the square in half like the tissue, repeat the same process as step 8. Scrunch the cellophane round the stems. (You can secure the cellophane with adhesive tape before adding the bow, although this spoils the effect to some extent.)

10 Using raffia to finish off this type of bouquet gives it an informal yet sophisticated look. Taking a few lengths of raffia, tie round the original binding point, and secure with a knot. Then make a bow by looping several strips of raffia round and round, pinch the loop in the middle and secure it on to the bouquet with the raffia already in position. Tease out the loops of raffia to make the bow fuller, and your gift bouquet is now complete.

HAND-TIED POSY

Regardless of the size of the finished piece, the principle of hand tying never changes. These days brides want more informal and natural flowers for their weddings, particularly for their bridesmaids. The following spring posy would be charming for any young bridesmaid to carry.

1 | Start the posy by making the required shape with the foliage; this is a fine-leaved eucalyptus. Remember to follow the principle of spiralling the stems without crossing them.

2 | Work the dainty stems of forget-me-not through the foliage, developing a good round posy shape.

3 | Muscari is so pretty, but as with all small flowers, it benefits from grouping in twos and threes, throughout the posy.

4 | The large-headed white ranunculus are better in single blooms over the whole piece. The posy is beginning to take shape now.

5 | Treat the bright red anemones in a similar way, arranging them in the spaces between the ranunculus.

6 | With all the flowers in place, you will need to tie the posy. Hold the posy with your left hand and wind twine or raffia three or four times firmly round the stems above your hand.

7 | Make sure you have left about 20cm (8in) of loose twine at the beginning and end to knot the ends together.

8 | Cut the stems level to the required lengths. As the posy will be held by a child, the stems can be cut quite short. Long stems can look ugly in the wedding photographs. Keep the posy in a small jug or vase in a cool place until it is needed for the occasion.

9 | A simple white satin bow is all you need to complete this delightful piece.

CANDLES

Flowers arranged with candles is a marriage made in heaven! Candles can enhance the simplest supper for two and add splendour to a banquet. The quality of light is mood-setting, gentle and flattering to flowers and faces.

There are so many types of candles available these days, but when combined with flowers, it is very important to select slow-burning, non-drip candles. You will always have to pay more for them, as they have a higher proportion of beeswax. Church candles, in particular, are worth the extra cost, as they burn slowly and evenly and have a beautiful quality of light.

It is essential to bear in mind that the candle cannot be allowed to burn down to its base, so try to find out the burning time of the candle and buy a slightly taller candle if necessary.

SECURING THE CANDLES Candles can be secured in the foam in a number of different ways. The simplest way is to push the candle directly into the foam, and this is quite satisfactory for slimmer candles. Alternatively, the candle can be fixed in a proprietary green plastic candle holder. However, these only really work if the candle fits snugly in the holder, although the wax can be trimmed if the diameter is too large, or you can wind sticky tape round the bottom if it is too small. To fix large church candles securely, see step 1 of Table Arrangement (opposite).

> **FURTHER INFORMATION**
> ☞
> Materials, page **10**
> Grouping, page **56**

TABLE ARRANGEMENT

This sort of arrangement is suitable for a formal dinner party or it can be made to sit on a side table, sideboard or hall table, in which case it will be a three-quarters arrangement. If it is going on a dining table, bear in mind the other items that will be going on the table when it is fully set, and scale it accordingly.

For this piece it is not necessary to use a decorative container, a plastic florist's bowl with one-third of a piece of wet foam secured with tape is all that is needed.

1 Prepare a large fat church candle with four little stick "legs" secured with florist's tape. Sit the candle on the foam, with the stick legs pushed securely into the foam.

2 Arrange some eucalyptus in the foam. This creates the shape and outline of your finished arrangement.

3 Sunflowers are very dramatic and need carefully positioning within the arrangement. You will only need a few, which should be arranged in clusters of two or three, rather than dotted around.

4 Other flowers to add are Dutch freesias and Aalsmeer gold roses to pick up the golden yellow of the sunflowers. The success of a similar arrangement depends on matching tonal values within the same colour range, for example a primrose yellow would have been quite unsuitable with the sunflowers.

CANDELABRA ARRANGEMENT

Wrought-iron candle holders are very popular, and offer a great deal of potential to flower arrangers with a little imagination. This is a 5-candle candelabra, and the centre candle is replaced with a green "candle cup", which sits in the candle slot. If you are using a grander silver candelabra, chrome "candle cups" are also available.

1 | Use florist's tape to secure a small amount of wet foam onto the centre candle cup. Then tape the cup with the foam in it round the middle branch of the candelabra for extra security. This will not show as the flowers will disguise the tape.

Set the candles in position first as it is essential to balance the flowers with the height of the candles. At the same time you must be aware that the candles will not remain at that height, and that as they burn they may come dangerously close to the flowers.

2 | Begin by arranging the foliage, creating a good basic outline. Arrange the foliage up to your finished height, but also trailing down, using naturally flowing stems; eucalyptus foliage is very flexible and can be encouraged to bend in the direction you want.

3 | The delicate flowing lines of the dendrobium orchid "Golden Showers" is used to full effect for the downward curve. Red "pygmy" amaryllis on short stems are the feature flower of the piece. They have thick hollow stems, so only a limited number can be pushed into such a small piece of foam. You may have to hollow out a hole in the foam with a stick before inserting the amaryllis.

4 To unite the yellow of the orchid and red of the amaryllis, add golden yellow spray roses, with very round buds heavily tinged with red. As the buds open the red is still evident on the petals. The sprays are on strong stems and are very easy to push into the limited amount of space now left in the foam.

COLOUR

It's difficult to talk about flowers without mentioning colour and the colour wheel. The wheel is formed from primary and secondary colours. Primaries are red, blue and yellow, while the secondary colours are orange, violet and green, created by mixing two primaries in equal amounts.

Although colour can be highly emotive and personal, using colour theory you can define certain combinations; for example red and orange are warm colours and blue and green are cool colours. Colours found on the opposite side of the wheel are known as complementary contrasts such as orange and blue, and colours next to each other such as purple and red are known as adjacent.

USING NEUTRALS Hues such as white and grey, and shades with black and brown, all known as neutrals, are not generally included in the wheel as they don't form part of the colour spectrum. However, neutrals are used regularly in combination with other colours to create a harmonious effect. Green, which in all respects is a secondary colour, is more like a neutral colour to the flower arranger since it has a cooling effect on hot colours and adds interest to a monochromatic combination.

▲ Orange and purple is not a combination for the faint hearted! The hot colours of the tulips and asclepias are cooled down by the deep purple irises.

▲ Orange and deep pink are almost adjacent on the colour wheel. Here they produce an unlikely but exciting combination.

▲ A monochromatic scheme of cool pinks relies on a combination of textures with interesting foliage to create a pleasing effect.

◀ Another monochromatic scheme from the warmer side of the pink hue which combines apricots and corals. Gerberas always make an impact and they come in a wonderful range of colours from the subtle to the garish.

▶ The fresh combination of yellow and blue is perfect for spring. Here blue hyacinths are combined with narcissi and tulips and grey-green eucalyptus foliage.

▶ This arrangement evokes crisp winter mornings and frost covered trees. Symbolically white flowers represent purity, for instance *Lilium candidum* which is also known as the Madonna lily.

The montage of moss, dried flowers, herbs and old pots is a composition in cool colours, even the roses are a cool pink.

White flowers never cease to please, and they always look crisp and fresh in combination with one or two other colours. As white always shows up well it is ideal for poorly lit areas.

The colour of the red and green fruit in this arrangement is intensified because the two colours are opposites on the colour wheel. The striking colours of this fruit pyramid are enhanced by the glossy skin of the fruit which catches the light.

CONDITIONING FLOWERS

Nothing is more disappointing than spending a great deal of money on flowers only to find that they wilt within a few hours of purchase. There can be any number of reasons for this, but if you follow a few simple principles, you should be able to enjoy the blooms for as long as possible.

What few people appreciate is that when the flowers arrive in a flower shop, particularly if they have come from abroad, they have had a long journey from the nursery to the retailer, via the auction house and the wholesale buyer.

Conditioning has only one purpose and that is to introduce water back into the flower's stem system after a period of drought. When a plant is cut the end seals up after about half an hour to conserve the water that is already in the stem. Then to keep the transpiration level to a minimum, ideally the flowers should be stored at a low temperature. This natural seal needs to be cut before the flower will take water up into its stem again. The stem will seal up any time it is out of water, so you should re-cut each time.

The treatment for different types of stem may vary, and a few of these are shown below. However, these days, after considerable research by the Dutch, the practice of smashing or hammering the bottom of stems, especially woody stems, is actively discouraged. Hammering the stems destroys the delicate stem tissue and its ability to take up water, and passes dead plant material into the vase water that can easily turn to bacteria. It is always better to use a sharp knife or scissors than a hammer and be well stocked with suitable clean buckets. Using flower food is also recommended.

LILIES If roses are the queen of cut flowers, then lilies must be the king! They may be a little expensive at certain times of year but they have an unsurpassable vase life, particularly the *Lilium longiflorum* variety. Their only drawback is the orange stain from the pollen, more apparent in some varieties than others. The *only* way to overcome the danger of staining clothes if they are going to be placed in a vulnerable position, is to remove the stamens by hand. Tilting the bloom slightly down, draw the pollen off with the thumb and index finger. Wipe your thumb and finger on a piece of kitchen paper and repeat.

As far as conditioning is concerned, a sharp-angled cut to the base of the stem and removal of all leaves that will be immersed or that are damaged, is all that is required.

TULIPS Tulips have a tendency to droop from the neck just below the head, which is exaggerated by the stem continuing to grow. To keep the stems as straight as possible, at least at the beginning, cut the base at a sharp angle either with a sharp knife or scissors, then wrap the whole bunch with newspaper or florist's shop paper and let them drink in a deep bucket for an hour or two. This works miraculously on sad looking tulips even after a couple of days in a vase.

ROSES Roses are the most capricious of flowers, so paying attention to their conditioning is essential. A good rose will have a vase life of about a week, but so often they can be a disappointment.

Generally speaking the more you pay, the better quality the rose. If you buy those short cheap bunches from roadside vendors, for instance, you will almost certainly be disappointed, so try to go to a good retailer who has a regular turnover and who can advise you on the lasting qualities of the roses they keep in stock.

To condition the flowers at home (if they have not been treated by the florist), you need to strip off all the leaves up to the point of immersion. Also it is a good idea to remove the thorns with a good sharp knife, such as a penknife or a vegetable knife. Holding the stem with the bloom towards you, take the knife with the blade flat against the stem, gently slide the sharp blade against the leaves and thorns. There is no need to

use any force as the sharpness of the blade will clean the stem. When all the stems are stripped, cut the base of the stem at as sharp an angle as possible, to allow the maximum amount of water into the stem tissue. Put the cut roses into deep buckets or vases of clean *hot* water. If the stems are still a little droopy, follow the tulip method and wrap them in paper.

ANEMONES Apart from cutting the freshly purchased anemones at a sharp angle, the secret to keeping them looking fresh is always to keep the vase well topped up with water, as they consume a great deal. If they are a little limp when you first buy them, put hot water in the vase to encourage them to perk up – this works a treat.

HYACINTHS As a rule of thumb, all bulb material should be cut at an angle above the white fleshy portion that has been growing below ground level, however some Dutch growers who supply their hyacinths with the remains of the roots still attached advise no cutting at all, just that you clean off the soil from the base. Whatever method you choose, hyacinths make marvellous cut flowers with excellent lasting qualities and a lovely scent. They are also the only flowers that are not affected by the slimy secretions of the narcissus family and can be successfully combined in an arrangement.

AMARYLLIS Amaryllis as pot plants have been around for a number of years, but in the last few years many Dutch growers have developed new varieties for the cut trade. They have an extremely long vase life (anything up to two weeks provided they are regularly deadheaded) and look very dramatic in modern interiors. They have two strange quirks – the base of the stem expands and splits and the neck becomes weak after a few days. To prevent the base from splitting, cut the stem at a sharp angle and bind the end with sticky tape. To keep the head up, carefully insert a length of garden cane through the hollow stem until it can go no further, then trim the end of the cane with sharp scissors.

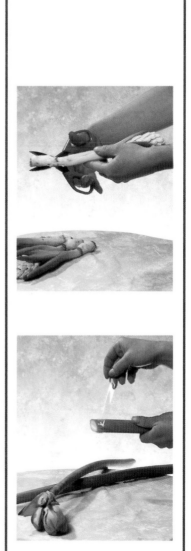

CONTAINERS

The container you use can be every bit as inspiring as the flowers. An old jug with splashes of bright colour, an elegant glass vase, an old-fashioned tin pitcher, watering cans, galvanized buckets, terracotta pots, chunky modern glass cubes, baskets in all shapes and sizes . . .

You can start a collection of containers for very little expenditure, and then you will always have the right container for the type of flowers, and when they aren't in use they make a decorative display on a shelf or in a cupboard. When selecting your container for a particular place, four points should be considered:

SPACE Ensure that you choose a container that will be in proportion with its surroundings when filled with flowers.

STYLE Try to choose vases or jugs that are in sympathy with the décor of the room or office.

COLOUR Choose a container that blends or contrasts with the colour scheme of the space.

FLOWERS Choose flowers that harmonize with the colour scheme and style of décor. In other words, the container and what eventually goes in it, is as much part of the décor as the curtains or carpets.

In an ideal world there is complete harmony between container, flowers and décor. However, in the real world you are much more likely to receive a bunch of flowers only to find that you simply don't have the right shape vase to do it justice. You will need to use all your ingenuity to make the best of this bunch.

If the bunch is too large for one container, spread it among one or two smaller vases. If the flowers are too short, use some scrunched up cellophane or chicken wire or marbles to prop them up in the vase.

MULTI-COLOURED JUG

This jug with its abstract hand-painted design has so many colours in it, and is such a classic style that it would fit in most informal settings.

1 Establish the overall finished shape of your arrangement with the foliage. Softly flowing eucalyptus leaves produce a pleasing outline, and rhododendron gives the centre a firm base.

2 As the general colour scheme is monochromatic, the flowers are not being grouped in this design. Starting with the roses, arrange the individual stems regularly through the piece.

3 Build up the design with the gerberas. Notice the soft grey green and cream of the *Euphorbia marginata*. Neither foliage nor flower, nevertheless it greatly adds to the overall scheme.

4 The delicate cluster heads of pale pink *bouvardia* complete this simple but effective arrangement. A piece like this is simple to make, requiring no fancy equipment or techniques, but would make a great impression in the right setting.

Jugs and vases, modern, traditional and antique, lend themselves to a variety of settings and inspiring flower arrangements. Glass vases look lovely on a bright windowsill, while jugs complement country kitchen tables.

Using a thirties-style glass
vase, a dramatic display in
oranges and magentas, with
trails of twisted stems, would
look very welcoming in an
office reception.

DESIGN

The two most important elements in the creation of a successful arrangement are design and colour. In approaching the subject of design, it should not be considered in isolation but as part of the three-dimensional world we all inhabit.

Look at the way objects in a man made or a natural environment are placed in relation to each other, whether it is a work of art, the arrangement of furniture in a room, or trees in a landscape. From these observations you can begin to identify the main elements that go to make up the spatial concept of design. They fall into the following loose categories: Shape or form, proportion and scale, texture, balance, contrast and finally rhythm. All these elements are in play when you are working with natural materials but it must always be your discerning eye that instructs your hands to make constant fine adjustments.

▲ This is a variation of the classic Victorian posy with its tightly constructed design using dried flowers and herbs instead of fresh flowers.

◄ The shape and form of this culinary sculpture is dictated by the materials used for its construction. If you are making an arrangement like this, it's essential to stand back from the piece every time you add more material to assess its balance.

▲ The distinct outline of this dried flower tree follows the traditional shape of a clipped bay or box tree found on formal terraces and parterres.

▲ This colourful jug of silk flowers is arranged in a loose but conventional way with the stems forming a simple and elegant fan shape. The eye is drawn to the handle of the jug which is balanced by the downward curve of the ivy trails.

▲ This is an example of a well-planned design that follows a rigid arrangement of contrasting shape, textures and colours for impact.

▲ Here is a good example of the English country style. It has a seemingly effortless quality that belies the careful positioning and balancing of the different shapes and textures of blooms and foliage.

▶ Another Victorian posy clearly showing the concentric rings of contrasting colours and shapes of the flowers, which is finished off with a circle of shiny pointed ivy leaves.

▶ This design succeeds because the proportions have been carefully considered. The shape of the solid base is repeated in the closely packed stalks of wheat. The focal point of the piece is the ring of fruit and flowers on the rim of the pot.

▼ This rose basket is a similar shape to the wheat in a flower pot design left, with the bunched roses echoing the outline and size of the basket.

▲ When designing an asymmetrical piece like this, consider not only the materials and their position within the group but also the space around the materials; this is what artists refer to as negative space. The aim when making parallel designs is to create a fine balance between line and mass.

Dried Flowers

There is a wonderful choice of dried flowers available now; the colour range is extended by dyeing and the introduction of freeze drying has introduced a range of large-headed roses and fruit that can be very inspiring.

The main stock of dried flowers is always commercially dried in kilns and the new season's stock starts appearing in early summer. Dried flowers are, of course, available all the year round, but the previous year's crop does start to look a bit faded by the spring. The best time to consider starting a dried arrangement is in the autumn. You may have had an opportunity to dry your own flowers during the summer so you could incorporate them with shop-bought varieties.

If you have dried your own flowers, you will be aware how much the bunches shrink. This is why they are relatively expensive and why you will always need more flowers than you thought to make your display. But once made you will have several months enjoyment from it.

Choosing Dried Flowers When selecting flowers for your arrangement, try to choose varieties that contrast in colour and texture. As dried flowers lack the lustre and movement of fresh flowers you have to find other ways to bring the flowers to life. Quite often what would not be considered a suitable colour juxtaposition, for instance pink and orange, can bring extra drama and depth to a dried arrangement. Experiment with interesting shapes and contrasting colours to produce a finished piece that is not just a "dried arrangement", but a work of art!

Further Information
☞
Parallel arrangements, page **58**
Wiring, page **114**

Rose and Marjoram Basket

There is a wonderful selection of dried and preserved flowers and foliage available now. Red roses combined with purple flowering marjoram give the finished piece a rich, luxurious look. Roses are always an absolute winner in dried arrangements because their wide range of colours and unique shape are retained very well in the drying process.

This way of arranging dried flowers combines a maximum of two to three varieties in large groups, with a "collar" of the same flowers around the rim of the container, with moss filling up the gaps where the foam may show.

1 Using special dry florists' foam, cut a piece to fit the basket snugly, pushing it firmly into place.

2 Use smaller wedges in the gaps to secure the main piece. Cover the foam round the rim of the basket with moss.

3 | You will probably need about a bunch and a half of roses depending on the size of the basket. Start arranging the stems in a parallel fashion, with the blooms level with each other. The finished height to the piece is very much an individual judgement; there are no true rules of thumb, although it is often said that the container should constitute one-third of the finished height and the flowers two-thirds. If in doubt about this, it is best to cut the flowers longer than necessary, and then step back from the composition to trim them accordingly. This sort of decision making in flower arranging is a learned skill, along with all the other techniques shown in this book, and will come naturally after a degree of practice.

5 | Now repeat the same process with the marjoram, filling up the gaps in the tall stems of roses with bunches of the herb, and also round the rim, alternating roses with marjoram.

4 | Add little clusters of roses between the stems of the taller roses and the rim of the container.

ROSES AND POPPY BASKET

A large twiggy basket like this needs to be balanced with robust shapes and colours, such as spiky steel blue globe thistles (*Echinops*), rich red roses and grey poppy heads, filled in with soft larkspur and catmint (*Nepeta*).

1 | Prepare the basket with enough dry foam for the quantity of flowers to be used, then pack moss in the gaps around the sides.

2 | The success of this arrangement relies on grouping the flowers in small bunches as you add them to the display. Wire the individual stems of roses together to make a compact bunch.

3 | Arrange the wired bunches of roses in the basket in a very upright manner, leaving space between the groups for the addition of the other flowers.

4 The design is beginning to take shape. Bunches of globe thistles, larkspur and catmint are grouped tightly together, with the tops of the flowers all finishing at the same level. The effect is rather like a clipped hedge.

5 Use the strong poppy stems to fill in any gaps left in the arrangement. Dried poppies have an organic quality which blend in well with this woody container. Their round bleached heads contrast beautifully with the strong colours of the other flowers.

FREE FORM SCULPTURE OR HANGING

All sorts of natural materials can be used as exciting additions to the usual flowers, foliage and dried flowers. When walking in the country or at the seaside, look out for suitable materials to include in your sculptures.

Shells, stones, driftwood, seaweed, pieces of moss, twigs and pieces of tree bark, and fungi (which dry beautifully on top of a radiator) are all ideal materials. In the autumn you can supplement these with gourds and an abundance of dried fruit and vegetables, including citrus fruit, chilli peppers, corn-on-the-cob, apple slices and pomegranates. For a touch of scent, gather bunches of rosemary, bay and thyme, hang them up for a few days, and when they are dry they can be incorporated into your culinary sculpture.

OTHER MATERIALS Using non-flower materials either for a permanent arrangement or sculpture, or with a fresh flower arrangement, is both economical and inspiring. All sorts of fabric remnants can be used in free form pieces if the colour and design is suitable. Potting sheds can also be a good source of interesting subject matter, and junk shops and street markets will provide lots of alternative cheap materials.

CULINARY SCULPTURE

This piece is designed to hang on the wall. The framework is a piece of ivy root (the ivy had been growing up a tree and these were the thick aerial roots clinging to its trunk).

1 Using the glue gun, stick a plait of garlic along a section of the root to form a pleasing curve. This creates the main line of the sculpture.

2 Glue on two or three stems of dried corn-on-the-cob.

3 Now glue on large pieces of fungi and stems of yellow pepper to make a pleasing arrangement.

4 Working up and down the ivy framework, add a dried cottage loaf, green and yellow chilli peppers and twirls of green tagliatelle to complete the sculpture. The piece is now ready to hang in a kitchen or in an informal dining room.

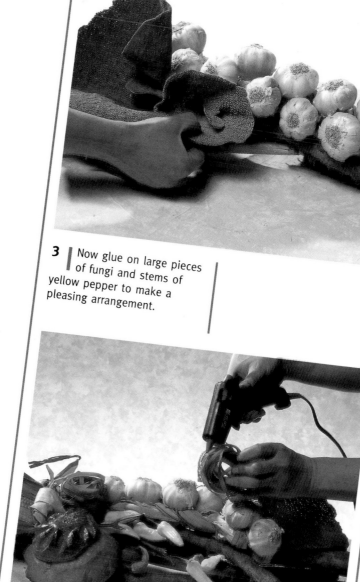

FRUIT AND VEGETABLES

The tradition of combining fruit and vegetables with flowers is not a new idea and can be observed in the Dutch and Flemish still life and flower paintings of the seventeenth and eighteenth centuries.

In Roman times, grapevine garlanding was used as decoration for great feasts, in honour of the god Bacchus. Today fruit and vegetables offer creative designers the same opportunity to combine the different textures of fruit and vegetables to enhance their flower arrangements. From the seventeenth century onwards, fruit and flowers were a constant source of inspiration for the decorative arts in textiles and wall coverings, when materials, wallpapers and ceramics were beginning to be imported into Europe from the Far East. Their use reached its apotheosis in the Victorian era with sumptuous dinner tables dressed with great cascades of fruit and bowls of flowers: the proud display of the country house kitchen garden.

SHOPPING FOR IDEAS   These days supermarket shelves offer the creative flower arranger almost as much inspiration as the flower shop and with more and more "designer" fruit and vegetables appearing in our shops, the ideas are unlimited! Grapes, particularly black varieties, always combine well with flowers, but other fruit and vegetables, from abundant autumn apples to the more exotic aubergines and figs, make wonderful additions to an arrangement for a special occasion. Even the lowly Savoy cabbage has a beautiful structure and would add an interesting and inexpensive textural quality to a design.

FURTHER INFORMATION
☞
Seasonal arrangements,
page **74**

FLOWERS, MUSHROOMS AND AUBERGINES

This novel use of vegetables combined with flowers would be very eye catching for a sophisticated buffet or supper party. There are so many combinations that can be made with all the exotic fruit and vegetables available in the shops these days. Most of the arrangements in this book show flowers displayed in their most natural form.

Sometimes it is a challenge to create something in which the flowers have to conform to a rigid design. In this piece the upright positioning and simple colour scheme emphasize the contrasting textures of the flowers and vegetables. The inspiration for an arrangement like this may come as much from the vegetables as from the flowers. To complement the upright design, use a tall basket that would usually hold a houseplant.

1 Fill the basket with foam and start arranging the tall, straight flowers, in this case claret-coloured stocks. Group them tightly together with the stems cut to equal length. You will not need any foliage for this design as the foam will eventually be covered by the flowers and vegetables arranged in graduated steps.

2 Having made a good solid clump in the middle of the basket with the stocks, the next level is formed by the white roses arranged like "soldiers" to hide the stems of the stocks.

3 As the success of this piece depends on the flowers and vegetables being placed in a neat regimented way, try to make sure that each stem is cut to the same length. Now take some claret-coloured freesias, which match the colour of the stocks, and tuck them in beneath the roses. Wire the mushrooms so that the tops and stalks alternate round the rim of the basket.

4 Wire the aubergines in the same way as the mushrooms and then push them into the foam above the mushrooms. It is best to leave the aubergines until last as they are heavy and need careful positioning. Push them in evenly round the design spacing them equally.

BYZANTINE PYRAMID

This spectacular piece is easier to make than it appears, and is certainly worth the effort as it would make a sensational centrepiece for a wedding or anniversary party. It is rather like one of those china fruit pyramids, and as the name implies, evokes luxury and opulence. The piece can be made with any fresh fruit available, but it is important to select fruit that can be secured firmly on to the foam with a wire. You will need a suitable container; select something plain that will complement the elaborate fruit design. A simple terracotta pot will look very good and provides a solid base for the pyramid construction. You will also need a combination of about 6–8 different fruits: green and red apples, green and black grapes, red pears, passion fruit (used cut in half), large strawberries and baby pineapples.

1 Build up blocks of soaked foam to the approximate finished height, securing them with two garden canes right through the middle to the bottom of the pot. Carve the foam to a rough cone shape.

2 For extra security, cover the foam with chicken wire, pressing it firmly on to the foam, keeping the cone shape.

3 Cover the foam and chicken wire with pieces of flat green "carpet" moss pinned on to the foam.

4 Gradually build up a good cone shape with the moss. You could use sphagnum moss, but if there are any gaps between the fruit, the carpet moss looks much more attractive.

5 Prepare all the fruit in advance, so that you can concentrate on positioning the pieces on the cone without having to stop. The larger pieces of fruit like apples and pears are better fixed with a short stick or a piece of garden cane pushed through the core, allowing about 7.5cm (3in) of cane to project from the fruit. To give the fruit a good finish, polish the skin with a soft cloth. Fix the heavier pieces of fruit on to the shape first working round the cone, adding the more delicate fruit last.

6 If you can find baby pineapples, they add a delightful touch to the arrangement. They can be ordered at certain times of the year from a flower shop, but they are also available in the exotic fruit section in supermarkets. The third pineapple will form the top of the cone.

7 Working evenly round the cone, fill in the gaps with little bunches of grapes, reserving a good bunch until last to hang informally over the rim of the pot.

GROUPING

Arranging flowers in groups is a device copied from nature, where flowers grow naturally in clumps of the same type. Rather than dotting one type of flower throughout the display, try bunching together two or three blooms, balancing them with the contrasting shapes and colours of other flowers and foliage.

This is a particularly effective method for showing off flowers which are small or delicate, for example tiny spring flowers such as narcissi, muscari or hellebore. In the summer, pinhead flowers like cornflower, nigella and astrantia look much more natural and have far more impact if they are grouped together.

CHOOSING THE COLOURS Generally speaking blue flowers recede, so by placing them closely together they will have more impact. This is worth remembering if you have to make a large piece for a church or hall, using lots of blue summer flowers such as larkspur and delphinium, which are so majestic but can be rather lost in a large display without careful planning.

When you are choosing your flowers for a grouped arrangement, as well as thinking about the colours, consider the contrasting shapes of the blooms and the foliage, and also the texture; for example waxy tulips with velvety roses.

> **FURTHER INFORMATION**
> ☞
> Colour, page **32**

CONTRASTS

This is an arrangement of strong contrasts. Firstly, the colours are taken from the opposite side of the colour wheel. Secondly, the hard lines of the container are contrasted with the flowing foliage. Thirdly, the flowers themselves – tulips, asclepias, lisianthus and trachelium – each has a unique texture which will be enhanced by contrast.

1 As this is an arrangement without foam or chicken wire, the foliage forms the base for anchoring the flowers in position. Arrange the foliage to the general shape you imagine the finished arrangement.

2 Arrange the two bunches of showy, waxy orange tulips in twos and threes all round the vase. When cutting tulips, bear in mind that they grow about a third more in length, so they should either be cut back down to size or cut shorter to allow for growth.

4 *Trachelium*, also a popular new variety, is composed of tiny clusters of purple-blue flowers in a flat head. A general rule of thumb is to place flat-headed flowers deep into the arrangement, rather like a filler. The heads of *trachelium* tend to be quite large so grouping as such is not necessary, however as there is some variation in head size, you may need to put a couple of smaller stems together.

3 Next add the beautiful bell-shaped *lisianthus* in deep purple. This flower is a fairly recent addition to the selection available in shops, but has become a firm favourite.

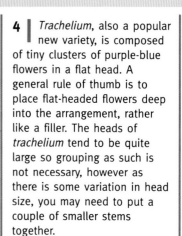

5 Now for the final touch. *Asclepias* is a vivid orange cluster-type flower, with a delicate arching habit. Group the stems together, cut them at a midway point between the *trachelium* and tulips, encouraging their natural arching tendency. As a final elegant touch, add some pieces of "bear" grass round the edge of the composition.

PARALLEL ARRANGEMENTS

Parallel designs were devised in Holland and probably took their inspiration from Japanese ikebana. They make use of interesting foliage shapes and colours, and sculptural twig forms such as contorted willow or witch-hazel.

Parallel arrangements need careful thought before beginning. Simplicity is at the heart of these sort of designs and the choice of flowers is crucial as fewer are needed than in a traditional arrangement. When selecting the blooms, do make sure that they are all perfect. You will probably only need three contrasting varieties and about three to five blooms of each type, some unusual foliage including large leaves, some "carpet" moss and an interesting twig.

These sort of pieces are usually arranged in shallow dishes, which will limit your choice of flowers to those on a sturdy stem. If the stems are a little lax you may need to wire them.

Designs like these are challenging to execute as they require tight control of the plant material. The placing of the flowers and leaves follows a formal pattern of vertical and horizontal lines, with the sculptural branch breaking through the formality to add rhythm and movement. This technique is most satisfying to practise as it requires a keen eye for design and artistic balance.

FURTHER INFORMATION
☞
Wiring, page **114**

PARALLEL DESIGN WITH IRISES

The choice of flowers for this piece, contrasts the rigidity of irises with the delicacy of dendrobium orchid "James Storey" and the round daisy face of the germinis. The colour scheme is simply orangey red and purple blue, enhanced by croton leaves. The dish is a shallow dark green china bowl with gold marbling. Fix a piece of foam in the bowl with florist's tape and secure it with moss to prevent any movement.

1 Push a piece of green (non-flowering) broom into the foam at the back, ensuring that it is upright, so as to establish the general height of the piece. Add a small bunch of laurel just in front of the broom, cut quite short. The two delicate pieces of contorted willow follow the horizontal and vertical lines.

2 To reinforce the horizontal axis, add the colourful croton leaves. It is best to wire the leaves so that they can be gently bent over the rim of the dish. Any sort of interesting leaves can be used – large variegated ivy leaves with splashes of cream are particularly attractive.

3 | Complete the vertical line with deep purple irises "Blue Magic". In this arrangement, separate the open from the closed irises. Take the closed iris stems and push them into the foam, keeping the stems very close to each other and varying the lengths only fractionally.

Position the group of open iris blooms at about half the height of the first group. Place them close together and arrange them so that as each bloom is cut it is fully displayed. In these types of arrangements, each flower must earn its keep in the design!

IKEBANA

The art of ikebana, meaning "living flowers", is influenced by the Japanese tradition of Zen Buddhism. This is a tradition that sees beauty in imperfection and impermanence.

The three main elements of any arrangement are:- *Shin*, representing Heaven and expressing the future: *Soe*, the middle line, standing for Man and the present: *Hikae*, the shortest line, representing earth and expressing the past. Every ikebana arrangement is a unique piece because it is the creation of its arranger.

4 | Place the orchids to complete the horizontal lines. On the left-hand side they follow the line of the willow. To place the orchid on the opposite side, draw an imaginary line from the tip of the stem already in place through the bowl following a line to the other side.

5 | The last flowers to add are the deep red germinis. Don't be afraid to cut them short, as they need to sit deep in the arrangement in a group below the open irises, the red contrasting strongly with the purple. The first two are arranged very close to each other, with a larger gap before the third. This last stem may need to be wired, as the large daisy heads of germinis do not always face the way the designer intends! When the last stem of flowers is added, fill any gaps with moss and top up the bowl with water.

PICTURES

With an empty wall, suitable materials and

inspiration you can achieve decorative pictures with a

three-dimensional effect. Your most valuable asset

will be a hot glue gun allowing

you to build up your designs and

to fix materials and flowers to

whatever surface you choose.

The simple but effective rustic montage demonstrated opposite is made with readily available natural materials on a card background. Another simple and satisfying project to decorate is a mirror. A flat-framed one without any moulding is ideal, but as the frame will be completely covered you can buy a cheap pine-framed mirror from a junk shop or from one of the many pine shops that seem to have proliferated in the last few years.

MATERIALS When you have chosen your background you can select the flowers and other materials for your piece: this can include driftwood, moss, twigs, old pots, gourds, dried fruit and fungi, and also lengths of fabric to wind through the composition.

PLAN YOUR DESIGN The design can either be a free form asymmetrical layout or it can follow a regular pattern. Arrange your selection of materials, then start working round the frame with the hot glue gun, making sure you cover it completely, and that each piece is securely fixed. If you are using fabric, wind it loosely through the composition, sticking it on to the frame at intervals. The fabric helps to tie the composition together visually, and is also very useful if you are a little short of other materials.

┌─────────────────────────────────┐
│   FURTHER INFORMATION   │
│   ☞   │
│   Equipment, page **8**   │
└─────────────────────────────────┘

RUSTIC MONTAGE

A raid on the garden shed (or the local garden centre) will produce most of what you need for this picture. It's fun to make, and once you've built up your confidence making the first, you'll probably have lots of ideas for more pictures.

1 Pierce two holes at the top of a piece of board or thick card and loop a piece of wire through to make a hanger. Cover the edges of the board with moss glued on with a general purpose adhesive, leaving space in the centre of the board for the pots and dried flowers.

2 Using a glue gun, glue four garden canes round the edge to make a "frame", overlapping the canes at the corners.

3 At each corner, tie the canes together with raffia, leaving an end of about 5cm (2in) to attach a raffia bow.

4 | To create a bow, make three or four loops of raffia, then pinch it in the middle, hold it on to the corner of the cane frame and tie it on with the raffia ties.

6 | Glue the flowerpots in position on the base board and cover the remaining board with moss.

7 | Now fill some or all of the little pots with bunches of flowers, such as dried roses and lavender which will smell lovely. Alternatively, you can fill them with seasonal flowers and change the contents of the pots during the year.

5 | For this picture, five 7.5cm (3in) Victorian terracotta garden pots add charm and rusticity to the composition, but plain modern terracotta flowerpots are almost as good. Any number of pots can be used, depending on the finished size of your board.

PLANTED GARDENS AND POT ET FLEUR

A ready-planted flowering arrangement makes a long-lasting present. While a Pot et Fleur, which means literally pot and flower, combines the longer-lasting qualities of potted plants with the beauty of cut flowers.

CONTAINERS If you want to make a planted arrangement in a permanent watertight container such as a terracotta trough or a china or glass bowl, it is a good idea to line the base with old pieces of broken crock for drainage. Always remember to water plants regularly and follow any instructions that come with the plants. Water can ruin highly polished surfaces, so it is probably best to take the container to the sink when watering and then dry it off before replacing. Pot et Fleur arrangements tend to be fairly temporary, so a basket lined with a bin liner is ideal.

COMPOSITION When choosing the plants, try to select them for contrasting shape and colour, and arrange the individual plants to create a composition, in the same way you would choose and arrange cut flowers for a fresh display. A few purely foliage plants can be incorporated into the design; ivies are particularly attractive with their trailing stems. When the flowering plants have long since finished, these green plants can be repotted, and if well cared for will eventually grow into sizeable houseplants.

PLANTED GARDENS

This sort of plain "laboratory" glass has been popular for a few years, especially in modern settings. The large cylinders look very effective with tall lilies, for instance, but these shallow versions can be a little tricky. If you can get hold of some attractive moss (it may be worth ordering from your local flower shop), you can transform the container and, with imagination, have a bit of fun.

1 Having acquired your moss, start lining the sides of the cylinder. Scatter the base with several pieces of broken crock (such as broken terracotta pots) for drainage. Alternatively, you can use clay pellets.

2 Half fill the space with fresh all-purpose compost, making sure the moss doesn't collapse into the middle.

3 This lovely cream splashed ivy will form the front of the finished design. Allow the trails to fan out. Plant two short red primulas each side of the ivy.

5 | Cover the compost and roots with more moss. Add some larger shards of terracotta to make an informal decoration on top of the moss.

6 | Large shells and pebbles collected from the beach also make an original and pleasing decoration.

4 | Place a *Primula malacoides* in between the shorter primulas. These delicate-looking members of the primula family come in many pretty colours from pure white to deep red. They are long lasting indoors but unsuitable for the garden. Hyacinths are lovely plants for the home, and as they will grow quite tall, they will look best at the back. In this particular case, the bulbs are more than half-grown, but if you want to use them less open your design must take their final height into consideration.

POT ET FLEUR

This is a novel idea for combining pot plants, flowers and foliage, with a section composed entirely of cut flowers. People are often saddened at the thought of throwing their expensive present away after a very short while, but with a Pot et Fleur, they will be able to enjoy the gift for much longer; the space occupied by the flowers can be replaced with more cut flowers or another plant.

For this particular arrangement a red miniature rose, coral-coloured primulas and ivy sit in the main basket, while the fresh arrangement fits into a similar but smaller basket.

1 Half fill the main basket with compost, then position the smaller basket (which is filled with foam) slightly off-centre on the compost. Once all the plants are in position, the small basket will sit quite firmly in place. Place the trailing ivy slightly to the side, and fill the small basket with foliage but leave the cut flower arrangement till last.

2 Take the plants out of their pots and arrange them to create a pleasing composition until the large basket is full. Make sure they are well tamped down, then fill up the gaps with extra compost.

3 All the colours for this composition are within the range of warm reds and corals, starting with orangy red alstroemeria. The tall alstroemeria stem usually has between 3–5 short stems at the top, each one carrying a bloom. Cut off the short stems and use them separately.

4 As the colours in this piece are carefully harmonized, you can introduce a large-headed flower like these apricot gerberas without difficulty. Cut them shorter than the other blooms as the large daisy shape tends to dominate.

5 | Just three or five richly coloured apricot roses are enough to give the piece a touch of luxury. Cut these longer so that they are not crowded by the gerberas.

6 | Fill in any remaining gaps with sprigs of pinky red waxflower to balance the design.

7 | Take some handfuls of beautiful springy carpet moss and pack it firmly round the plants to disguise the compost. You should be able to get moss from a florist or garden centre. Sphagnum moss is also suitable for this purpose.

PRESERVING AND DRYING FLOWERS

Buying preserved and dried flowers and foliage from a specialist shop can be very expensive so why not try drying some flowers yourself? The time to start is when fresh flowers are plentiful in the garden and also relatively cheap in the shops.

There are several ways of drying and preserving flowers and foliage; however some methods are not suitable for drying at home.

FREEZE-DRYING is a relatively new commercial process which requires expensive equipment but produces wonderful results especially with large-headed flowers such as roses and peonies. Vegetables also freeze-dry very successfully and can be used in a variety of designs.

PRESERVING IN GLYCERINE is an excellent method for preserving foliage, particularly eucalyptus and beech. Just put the stems in a bucket quarter filled with glycerine (or anti-freeze) for about a week. You will find the foliage takes up the glycerine and retains its pliability. The best time to use this technique is in the spring when the sap is rising.

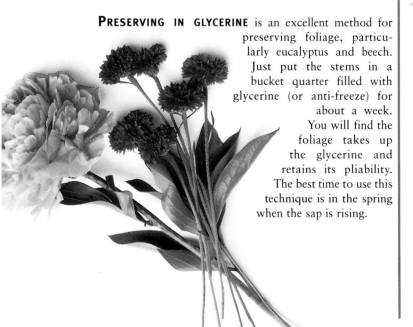

▲ Drying by natural evaporation is achieved by leaving the flower on its stem in the vase until all the water has evaporated. This method is ideal for drying hydrangea heads. The time to pick a hydrangea for drying is when the petals have matured and feel "leathery" to the touch. Avoid cutting the pale colours as these are not mature enough; the heads really need to turn deep russet or green before they can be cut for preserving.

▼ This rustic arrangement of hydrangeas, love-in-a-mist seedheads, larkspur and sea lavender is extremely simple but very effective. All of these flowers and seedheads can be air-dried.

KILN-DRYING Huge quantities of flowers are processed on a large scale by this method.

DRYING IN A MICROWAVE OVEN is suitable for preserving individual blooms such as hydrangea and sedum, and for drying leaves. Spread the flowers and leaves on a piece of kitchen paper on the microwave turntable. Cover with two or three more sheets of kitchen paper to absorb the moisture. Dry them on the lowest setting for about six or seven minutes.

▶ Air-drying is the simplest and most convenient method. Ideally, you will need a dark, dry and airy room or an airing cupboard for quicker results. Wire hangers from the dry cleaners are ideal for hanging bunches. In preparation for hanging, tie 8–10 stems of fresh flowers (don't give them a drink) with an elastic band, then push a heavy wire 1.25mm (18g) through the bunch, give it a quick turn and then form it into a hook to hang on the hanger.

▶ Drying in silica gel is an excellent method for delicate blooms with less colour fading than other methods. It is also suitable for drying spring bulb flowers such as narcissi. The gel can be ordered from chemist shops and although it is expensive it can be re-used by gentle baking in the oven. Sprinkle a layer of gel into a shallow dish and arrange the flower heads and leaves in a single layer on top. Sprinkle over more gel to completely cover the flowers. The crystals turn blue when they have absorbed moisture from the flowers, usually after about 24 hours, depending on the size of the bloom. The results of this method are excellent and the flowers look almost fresh, but it is more time-consuming than other methods and the container limits the size and number of blooms that can be treated in a session.

◀ Seedheads and grasses are good candidates for air-drying, but you might want to try silica gel for the roses. Gold craft powder gives an exotic touch to the lotus seed-pods.

Ribbons and Bows

There is now a wonderful selection of ribbon material available from flower shops, department stores, fabric shops and specialist gift shops. The array can be quite dazzling from rich coloured velvets and organdie to natural textured paper and sinamay, printed satins, elaborate flocked designs, gold and silver thread, and special seasonal designs for Christmas.

The last few years have seen the increasing use of ribbons with wire edging, particularly on softer, finer fabrics, which allow the bow maker to create a well-shaped bow that holds its shape without flopping. Wire-edged ribbons tend to be more expensive, but are certainly worth the extra as they will finish off a design with real panache. They especially come into their own at Christmas for trimming the tree, making wreaths and table decorations.

MAKING A FOUR LOOP BOW

This may seem tricky at first, but once mastered, bow making will give you the opportunity to trim things to a professional standard. The principle of making a bow is to tie the ribbon in a basic "figure of eight".

Start with a four loop bow as shown here, practise this until you feel confident, then you can add on any number of extra loops to create a really luxurious bow. Begin with a ribbon with enough "body" to hold its shape but soft enough to gather easily. To make a four loop bow you will need approximately one metre (1yd) of ribbon and a shorter length of about 26cm (10in) to tie the bow in the middle.

1 Taking one end of the ribbon, allow enough to form the "tail" of the bow, then holding the ribbon between thumb and forefinger, begin to form the first loop of the figure of eight.

3 | Take the ribbon in the opposite direction to form the second loop, repeating the same procedure as step 2.

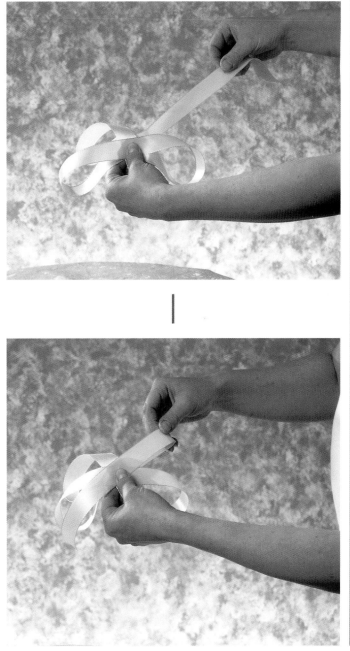

2 | Bring the ribbon back to the first hand (which hand goes where depends on whether you are left or right handed), to complete the loop, holding both pieces of ribbon between thumb and forefinger.

4 | The third loop is made by folding the ribbon diagonally to the first loop, and the fourth loop diagonally to the second loop, always returning the ribbon to the middle to be held by thumb and forefinger.

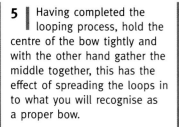

5 Having completed the looping process, hold the centre of the bow tightly and with the other hand gather the middle together, this has the effect of spreading the loops in to what you will recognise as a proper bow.

7 Your bow is now complete; all that remains is to pull the individual loops gently apart to improve the overall shape.

6 Holding the middle of the bow firmly, take the spare piece of ribbon with the other hand and tie firmly round the gathered loops in the middle of the bow.

TWO LOOP PAPER BOW

This useful bow can be made up in advance and used to decorate garlands and wreaths. The pleated paper ribbon is about 8cm (3in) wide and is flexible and easily shaped and available in many colours from a wide number of shops including the gift stationery departments in stores.

The loops are tied together in the middle with a length of wire, which holds the centre securely and is then ready to be attached to whatever you are decorating.

1 Follow the looping process described in steps 1, 2 and 3 of the four loop bow to form a two loop bow, then take the length of wire (about 36–40cm/14–16in) and wind it firmly round the middle of the bow, twisting one end of wire round the other to secure it.

2 Cover the centre with a short piece of paper ribbon to disguise the wire and tie this behind the bow.

SEASONAL ARRANGEMENTS

The year-round availability of unseasonal flowers at the florists has made a big impact on flower arranging. Traditional spring flowers like narcissi and tulips are available for at least six months of the year, and high summer flowers like larkspur and antirrhinum can now be found all year round.

This makes the idea of creating a truly seasonal piece all the more attractive. For instance, there are the contrasting blues and soft pinks of summer and the bright, almost clashing colours of autumn. Christmas is a season with its own rich palette and traditional materials to choose from. Spring flowers are a complete contrast to the rest of the year with their delicate shapes, colours and fragrance.

CHOOSING YOUR CONTAINER For a seasonal arrangement you should consider where you are going to place it, and make sure it is suited to the flowers of that particular season. For instance, an old terracotta pot is a wonderfully evocative piece for an autumn arrangement on a hall table, and a small, much-loved china bowl or jug would make a delightful container for spring flowers. Victorian-style flowerpots make versatile containers for all seasonal flower arrangements.

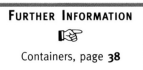

> **FURTHER INFORMATION**
> 👉
> Containers, page **38**

SPRING ARRANGEMENT

In our gardens and parks brave little snowdrops and crocuses are the first flowers of the new season. These can make a beautiful display in pots for the house as an early reminder that winter doesn't drag on for ever. In the local flower shop, however, seasons are stretched to such an extent that tulips are still available in summer and paperwhites in autumn, giving us six months of spring!

2 These lovely "Monte Carlo" tulips develop into large double heads, with good lasting qualities. Don't forget you may have to cut them again in a couple of days.

1 Fill the bowl with enough scrunched-up chicken wire to make a firm base for the arrangement. Top up the container with water. Use the stems of eucalyptus foliage first to form the required size and shape.

3 One of the great delights of this season is the scented flowers and no other flower can compare with hyacinths for fragrance. They are also extremely long lasting.

4 The dainty heads of forget-me-nots make a good filler and give this piece an informal feeling. Try to arrange them in clumps to make more impact.

5 Arrange these pre-cut orange-centred narcissi informally around the display.

TIPS

As spring flowers can be a bit tricky to arrange, here are a few tips to make it easier:

● Avoid using foam if you can, as it is very difficult to push in soft bulb flower stems. Instead, scrunched-up chicken wire in a container filled with water is far more suitable.

● Spring flowers bend and twist towards the light, and in the case of tulips and muscari, they actually continue growing. Try to allow for this in your arrangement.

● All members of the narcissi family produce a runny "sap" that contaminates other flowers. You can overcome this by cutting the stems to the required length, leaving them in water separately for about half an hour. Don't cut them again as the sap will reappear.

● Hyacinths may need some support through their hollow stems if they are a bit flaccid. Push a short wire or stick gently through the hollow stem up to the head.

6 Creamy white "Ice Follies" daffodils, also cut in advance, complete this colourful, fragrant arrangement.

SUMMER ARRANGEMENT

When the temperature rises, the cool colours of summer flowers can be as refreshing as a glass of iced tea. Some of the loveliest flowers appear in gardens and shops at this time of year: tall spires of delphinium, large globes of peonies, delicate scented sweet peas, antirrhinum, larkspur and lots of beautiful lilies. Such abundance makes the choice difficult. Take your inspiration from the garden if you have one, or from one that you enjoy visiting. You may be able to pick a few stems from your own garden without leaving obvious gaps; in fact, roses grow more abundantly if you keep picking them. You may also find some unusual foliage to add interest to your arrangement. Hosta leaves are especially prized by flower arrangers (if the slugs don't get them first).

1 ▎ Arrange the foliage first to create the outline and to make a firm base for the flowers as you will not be using any foam or chicken wire.

2 ▎ Aconitum, a perennial closely related to delphinium, has navy blue flowers in the shape of a monk's hood, hence its common name. Place them in a gentle fan shape following the line of the foliage.

3 ▎ Add strong stems of white antirrhinum to follow the general fan shape of the aconitum and foliage.

4 ▎ *Phlox paniculata* is a relatively recent addition to the cut flower trade, but has long been a favourite amongst gardeners. It is a later flowering variety in the garden, but is available in shops for an extended season from early spring to late autumn.

6 Continue to add flowers and foliage until the arrangement looks balanced and well-proportioned.

5 With their characteristic trumpet shape, lilies have the effect of drawing the eye into the centre of the arrangement. As a rule of thumb, when using any large-headed or eye-catching flowers, position them around the middle of the piece. These are known as "focal" flowers, a term much used by professionals and flower arrangers.

AUTUMN ARRANGEMENT

In tune with the autumn colours a beautiful handmade Victorian garden pot is ideal. Keep your eyes open for these versatile containers: it is possible to find modern hand-thrown pots which are equally attractive, although naturally they don't have the patina of age. Dried wheat, either green, or stone colour as here, is widely available and makes an inexpensive and appropriate material. The finished piece would make a lovely harvest festival arrangement.

3 | Pomegranates, with their orange-coloured skin and red flesh are very seasonal. To wire the fruit, push a 30cm (12in) florist's wire into the pomegranate, fold the ends back and push them into the dried moss on the rim of the pot.

1 | To start the arrangement you need about four or five bunches of dried wheat. Leaving the elastic bands on, trim the stems to make them level and cut all the bunches to the same length. Pack the bunches together, pushing them down into the pot, and filling the gap with dried moss.

2 | For the individual blooms of amaryllis use small water vials from florists. They are usually used for transporting delicate flowers such as orchids and they make ideal individual "vases" for single blooms. Snap off the amaryllis blooms, a stem usually has three or four blooms, and put each one into a vial, then push it into the moss.

4 | Halved pomegranates, with their shiny regular seeds, are even more attractive than the whole fruit. Wire them in the same way as the whole fruit, and arrange around the rim of the pot.

5 Push small orange-red roses and sprigs of cotoneaster berries into the vials and arrange in the moss to complete the arrangement.

WINTER ARRANGEMENT

This is a simple piece highly evocative of winter, which would look very dramatic in a candlelit room at Christmas time, and would make a great change from the usual reds and golds. The modern vase has a frosted finish which enhances the wintry atmosphere.

1 Larch is the only conifer to shed its needles, leaving attractive branches, covered with clusters of miniature cones. Arrange arching branches of larch, in a gentle fan shape.

2 If you can get hold of some cottonwool stems (these are available in some shops at Christmas time) they can be most effective to add to this sort of piece.

3 Beautiful long stems of cut hyacinth will make the room smell lovely and you will probably only need three stems for this arrangement. In Scandinavia, Christmas would not be complete without hyacinths.

4 Delicate trails of Italian genista (florist's broom) look like hoar frost and complete the icy effect.

SMALL SCALE

As you develop your skills with flowers, you will progress from the simple vase arrangement to pieces which emphasize the beauty and fragility of the individual blooms of a flower stem and also give you an opportunity to use the more advanced skills needed for fine work on a small scale.

Designs on this scale are invariably for special occasions, most obviously weddings, which may call for several small-scale pieces including buttonholes, corsages, hair decorations and cake decorations. As the finished work may be worn on lightweight clothing, it needs to be made with great delicacy, usually with wired flowers and leaves, so it's best not to tackle these particular items until you are sure of the the techniques.

FURTHER INFORMATION
☞
Wiring, page **114**

CAKE DECORATION

When you are considering making a piece to go on top of a tiered wedding cake, remember that most people's attention will be on the cake not the flowers, so they should never overwhelm it. A traditional wedding cake is usually an intricate affair of rosebuds, bows and garlands, so your crowning glory should set all that delicacy off to perfection. Your choice of flowers will mostly be dictated by the other flowers at the event and the colours and decorations on the cake itself.

1 You will need only the smallest piece of foam for this piece. There is a proprietary container available which is perfect for the job called an "igloo" (available to order from good flower shops).

It's always a good idea to find out the size of the top tier of the cake. Start by arranging the foliage to these dimensions.

2 Muscari are perfect small-scale flowers, with their delicate blue clusters. Arrange them in groups evenly round the piece.

3 Chrysanthemums would not be a first choice for a wedding piece, but these recently developed lime green miniature pinheads are very attractive and contrast so well with the strong coloured roses.

4 You will only need about five stems of roses. Cut them quite short and push them deep into the foam.

5 Little trails of jasmine, or any pretty trailing stems, make a charming finishing touch to the arrangement, cascading gently over the sides of the cake.

ROSE BUTTONHOLE

This simple piece uses all the techniques you will need when tackling more complicated designs. You should start with a good selection of wires and stem tape to bind the finished work.

1 Cut the rose right down, leaving just over 6mm (¼in) of stem. Push a 22 gauge (0.71mm) stub wire firmly up the stem, then inserting one end of a silver wire into the calyx, wind the wire round the rose stem and down the stub wire. Starting beneath the calyx, bind the whole length with stem tape.

2 For the backing you need three unblemished ivy leaves. To wire a leaf, thread a silver wire through the leaf vein, back down the stem forming a double leg mount. Choose a little piece of something delicate such as waxflower, to add interest. Wire the waxflower and tuck in at the side of the rose with one ivy leaf.

3 Now frame the flowers with the remaining wired ivy leaves. Cut the wires to length, allowing about 6cm (2¼in) of wired stem and bind with the tape to make a neat finish.

HAT DECORATION

Decorated with flowers, a plain straw hat can be transformed into something that would do justice to a day at the races or to a smart summer wedding. This hat is decorated with a large white phalaenopsis orchid with freesia, lysimachia, jasmine and ivy leaves as trimmings. However, a cluster of full-blown garden roses or a few open peony heads would look equally effective on a hat with a large brim. A flower-trimmed hat should make a statement, so avoid those shrinking violets!

1 The natural straw-coloured hat came with a dull brown band, which has been replaced with a smart white satin ribbon. Decorating a hat follows the same principles as making a corsage, and requires the same process of wiring and taping.

2 | Wiring the orchid is a bit tricky as the stem is at an awkward angle from the "face of the flower". Push the silver wire through the stem as near to the bloom as possible and, making a double leg mount, twist the wire round the stem and down. Finish the stem and wire off with tape.

3 | Dark green shiny ivy leaves will make a strong contrast with the flowers and a firm background for the design.

4 | These bright yellow freesias pick up the colour in the centre of the orchid and make a good contrast with its flat shape. Freesias are often used in small scale pieces as they have a delicate scent and a dainty appearance; they also hold up very well when wired and taped.

5 | Insert the wired freesia behind the orchid and in front of the ivy leaf. Use the lysimachia to balance the freesia by allowing it to curve gracefully the other way.

6 | Gradually build up the design to form a balanced composition of contrasting shapes and colours. Finish off the piece with some jasmine, or a piece of fern, gypsophila or September flower would be just as effective.

7 | Once you have assembled the wired and taped pieces, trim wires and bind them with stem tape.
When all the wires on the stem are well covered with tape, you are ready to attach them to the band on the hat. It may be easier and more secure to sew the decoration directly on to the hat with some neutral coloured thread.

Swags and Garlands

Garlands and swags are highly decorative pieces designed to hang on a wall or to enhance an architectural feature of a room such as an archway or fire surround. They can be a permanent feature made with dried material, or with fresh flowers and foliage for a one-off special occasion such as a wedding or an anniversary. At Christmas time fresh evergreens are perfect for combining with decorative festive materials such as ribbon, cones and other decorations.

Carved in stone and marble, swags and garlands were used throughout early classical times as architectural embellishments. The great seventeenth-century master of carved swagging and garlands was Grinling Gibbons, whose intricate work incorporating fruit, flowers and leaves is still a source of inspiration for designers.

When creating a floral garland or swag, allow yourself plenty of time as it will almost certainly take you longer to make than you anticipate, it will also take more foliage than you imagine, so be generous, especially with fresh material where you may be working against the clock.

> **FURTHER INFORMATION**
> ☞
> Wiring; page **114**

FRESH GARLAND

It is best to tackle this fresh flower garland in two stages: first make the foliage base, then when you are sure the length is right, add the flowers. The basic foliage for this garland is box, which is cheap, freely available all year round and easy to use. You can also add any other foliage that is seasonal and plentiful, but make sure that it will stand being out of water for a length of time. Break the pieces of box into small clusters in advance, so that you can form the garland quickly. Box leaves look much richer if you spray them with an aerosol plant leafshine. Depending on the length of the garland and where it is to be displayed, you can either make up the piece on a worksurface and position it when it is completed, or secure the foliage base and work on it in situ.

1 Start off with a ball of parcel string and some mossing reel wire. Leaving about 15cm (6in) of spare string at the end, start attaching the sprigs of box on to the string with the wire, making a double loop over the box and string. As the garland will only be seen from the front, you need not worry about the back which will lie flat against the wall.

2 Continue wiring the box in place, overlapping the bunches along the string. Every time you add another piece of box, it will conceal the string and wire. Complete this stage before you add the flowers.

3 Choose an open head from a stem of lily and wire and tape it using 35cm (14in) length of 20 gauge wire. Allow the lily to nestle in the foliage then pull the wire through to the back of the garland.

4 Support the garland with one hand, using the other hand to bend the wire from the lily back over the string, squeezing it firmly in place.

5 Start building up your design with the other flowers. Don't be put off by assuming you will need great quantities of flowers: just a few stems of lilies, roses and freesias simply arranged in regular clusters along the garland is all that is needed.

6 Repeat step 4, pushing the wired and taped flowers into the foliage. Once the piece begins to build up you will see that even a simple arrangement of a few clusters of flowers is extremely effective.

DRIED FLOWER HANGING

This is a quick and simple method for making a hanging and requires very few materials. You will need a big bundle of raffia to make the base for the hanging, then a selection of three different and contrasting dried flowers. For this hanging you will need to make in advance about four small wheat and marjoram bundles; cut them short and tie them firmly with raffia.

2 | Gradually work down the length of raffia and tie the bottom off with another piece of raffia.

3 | Attach the prepared bunches of natural wheat to the plait with lengths of raffia, with all the heads facing down.

1 | Firmly tie a good handful of raffia at the top with a piece of raffia, then divide the bunch into three sections, and start to plait it.

4 Tie on the wheat bunches so that they zigzag all the way down the raffia plait.

5 Tie the small marjoram bunches on to the raffia plait in front of the wheat bunches, in the same direction as the wheat.

6 As focal flowers add the bright pink peonies to the little wheat and marjoram clusters using groups of about 3 stems per cluster. Simply cut the stems down to about 4cm (1½in) and tuck them in to the plait; they should hold quite firmly, but you can use a hot glue gun to secure them if necessary.

TABLE ARRANGEMENTS

Even a few flowers gathered from the garden on the spur of the moment will make a table set for a small party look more inviting. No matter how informal the occasion, it's always worth setting some time aside to dress the table with flowers; the food will look more appetizing and you may get twice as many compliments from your guests.

No matter what the occasion, a few points are worth bearing in mind when making an arrangement for your table:
• The finished shape should reflect the shape of the table.
• The colours should tone in with the decor of the room and the china and linen.
• The scent should not be too overbearing.
• The finished height should not interfere with the guests' view of each other.
And finally your choice of flowers will depend on the occasion, season, budget and menu.

ARRANGEMENT FOR A HALL TABLE

This piece is designed to be seen from the front and to fit in with any other pieces you may usually keep on your hall table.

1 Fill the vase with wet florist's foam then start to shape the arrangement with the eucalyptus leaves. Eucalyptus has a natural arching habit, which can be encouraged with a gentle bend of the stem. Try to place each piece of foliage to follow its natural direction of growth, so that a stem placed to the right of the arrangement curves that way, and vice versa.

2 Spring flowers can be a little difficult to arrange because of their soft stems, but paperwhites have relatively strong stems once they have had a good drink. In any case, if you use them first you will find it easier as there will be more space in the foam.

3 | Guelder rose, properly known as *Viburnum opulus* 'Sterile', is a common hedgerow shrub, also available in a number of improved garden varieties. The Dutch grow several kinds of long-stemmed spring-flowering shrubs as well as viburnum, such as lilac, forsythia and almond blossom, which are also available long before their natural season. The attraction of this viburnum is its early lime green stage which gradually fades to cream.

5 | Part of the same family as anemones and buttercups, ranunculus have characteristic double "tissue paper" petals with a fresh green centre. The ranunculus and tulips form the focal point to this arrangement.

6 | Add a few sprigs of white waxflower to add softness and delicacy to the piece. Filler material like waxflower, September flower, statice or gypsophila, should always be used in moderation and never allowed to swamp or mask the main flowers of the design.

4 | These beautiful double-centred cream tulips are a recent addition to a species that is second only to roses in its dazzling variety. Choosing from such a choice of shapes and colours can be extremely difficult! Don't forget to make allowance for the tulips to continue to "grow".

DINNER PARTY ARRANGEMENT

Flowers in the centre of a dining table can be almost as much of a talking point as the food, so choose them with care, perhaps taking an idea from the décor in your room or the tablecloth fabric to influence your choice of flowers. In this particular case the inspiration for the decoration came from the design on the 1940s Royal Doulton china.

1 | Tape a piece of florist's foam, about a third of a "brick", on to a florist's plastic bowl. Now begin to form your basic shape and overall size with the foliage. As this arrangement is for an oval table, try to create a soft "diamond" shape with the greenery.

TIPS

If you are planning to make a table arrangement for a dinner party, try to follow a few simple tips:

● The shape of the arrangement should reflect the shape of the table.

● Make sure the piece does not take up too much valuable space.

● Keep the decoration low enough for the guests to be able to see each other across the table.

2 | The focal flower for this piece is a single stem of creamy white amaryllis, from which individual blooms have been carefully broken off. As they are very fragile it is best to put them in at the beginning while there is plenty of space in the foam.

3 | To make the arrangement pointed at each end, it's a good idea to select flowers that taper naturally, like these elegant miniature gladioli. Unlike their larger, rather ungainly, cousins, small gladioli are extremely versatile and come in a selection of lovely colours.

4 | If purple-blue irises are a bit too closed, you can encourage them to open out a little by teasing them gently apart. Arrange two stems near the centre on the diagonal, then add two at each end cut just a bit shorter than the gladioli.

5 | Cheerful red tulips pick up the red on the china and add to the general spring-like feel of the piece.

6 | Don't waste the tulip leaves, but select the best ones to add texture and contrast to the piece. The leaves will still have some of the stem which you can use to push into the foam.

7 | These bright yellow freesias also follow the colour scheme of the china and their dainty heads contrast well with the iris.

8 | Add a little touch of luxury to the occasion by using a few roses; you will only need 3–5 stems for a decoration of this size.

Topiary and Flower Trees

Topiary is a term borrowed from gardening, in which box, bay and yew hedges are clipped into shapes, either as free-standing pieces or as part of a hedge. Here a simple pompon has been used for inspiration.

Indoor topiary or flower trees can be made in any size – a tall pair in Versailles planters to stand in a grand entrance hall, or a miniature moss tree to sit on a side table or on a mantelpiece. Full-size trees with fresh foliage and daisies look very effective at the entrance to a wedding marquee.

Making Your Tree Whichever type of tree you choose, the technique for fixing the stem remains the same. Choose a steady-based container, then find a smaller plastic pot to fit snugly inside it (eg a yogurt pot). Select a suitable natural material to form your stem: cinnamon sticks, a small branch, or several twigs strapped together with raffia or string.

To fix the stem in the lining pot, you will need plaster of Paris. This is easy to use and sets within 40 minutes. Just mix the plaster, to make sufficient to fill the liner; it need not fill the pot right to the top. Place the stem in position and pour in the plaster packing it in quite firmly, holding it for a few minutes until it is self supporting and then leave to set. It will be ready to take its "topping" within 40 minutes.

FURTHER INFORMATION

☞

Wiring, page **114**

FRESH FLOWER TREE

Taking the topiary idea one step further, you can create these flower trees in all sizes for any special occasion. They are simpler to make than you may imagine, selecting suitable materials being the essential factor. For instance, it's best to select round or flat headed flowers, rather than the spiky varieties as these detract from the clipped look of a topiary tree.

1 The stem for this fresh tree is a combination of fresh and dried flower stems tied together securely with raffia. Push a square of soaked florist's foam firmly onto the trunk.

2 To get the initial pompon shape use fresh hydrangea heads. Break the heads up into smaller clusters, working all over the foam, to gradually build up the shape. You could use other seasonal fillers instead to cover the foam.

3 Then place bright red "germini" (miniature gerbera) regularly into the foam, always taking care that they nestle into the filler material at the same level so as to maintain the ball shape.

Sometimes the stems of the germini may be a little weak, in which case push a wire up into the stem as an extra support.

4 Place small open-headed orange-red roses in the spaces between the germinis to add texture and to intensify the colour. Add them in clusters rather than dotted around to contrast with the single daisy effect of the germini.

DRIED FLOWER TREE

This follows the same principles as the fresh tree, but uses all dried materials .

1 The trunk for this piece has been made from a bunch of large cinnamon sticks set in plaster of Paris. To add texture, wind some string around the pot. Secure the end with a blob of glue and keep winding round the pot until you achieve a pleasing finish, then push the end of the string under a loop to secure it. You can also add texture to a new pot by spraying it lightly with paint, or rubbing plaster of Paris into the terracotta. Lightly pack some fresh green moss around the stem to cover the plaster.

2 Push a square of dry foam firmly down onto the trunk, stretch a piece of chicken wire round it and secure underneath. The wire will be the base for the moss.

3 Pin "carpet" moss, onto the foam with "hairpins" of stub wire, to gradually transform the square into a pompon. You can add extra moss to improve the shape as you work round the piece.

4 Lotus pods are the focal decorative material of the tree. The shape of the pods enhances the overall roundness of the pompon. Push a piece of wire through the back of the pod and fold the ends back, then push it firmly through the moss into the foam.

5 Continue adding pods all over the foam and moss base until you have a pleasing ball shape. Step back now and again to check your work.

6 Now use poppy heads to fill in the gaps left by the lotus pods, packing them in tightly. They are easy to buy and fairly inexpensive, so they make an excellent filler.

7 Add clusters of dried red roses, in groups of two or three in the remaining spaces. Although dried roses are expensive, they are worth using as they have such a rich colour and add a luxurious finish.

8 To finish off the base, add a few poppy heads and roses to the moss to give an informal touch to the piece.

REINDEER MOSS TREE

All the inspiration for this piece came from the beautiful section of tree branch covered in moss and lichen.

1 Secure the branch in the usual manner and pack in position with lots of spongy "reindeer" or lichen moss.

2 As a decorative touch tuck dried orange segments down between the moss and the glass container.

3 Push a block of dry foam onto the trunk, cover it with chicken wire then lay the sphagnum moss base over the foam and tie it on tightly with reel wire. Add a little bundle of moss around any projecting branches.

4 Using "hairpins" of wire, pin reindeer moss over the sphagnum moss to cover. Fill up the pot with more moss, which will harden as it dries to form a secure base.

For a small moss tree, fix a tree branch into a pot with plaster of Paris. Make a ball of fibrous sphagnum moss and bind it tightly with reel wire onto the branch. Now pin green carpet moss onto the ball of moss with "hairpins" of wire. Finish off the top of the pot with carpet moss to hide the plaster.

TUSSIE MUSSIES AND VICTORIAN POSIES

The carrying of small posies, also called tussie mussies, can be traced back to Elizabethan times, when ladies would carry a small nosegay of sweet-smelling herbs such as lavender and rosemary to ward off unpleasant smells emanating from the city streets.

By the nineteenth century, the range and availability of decorative flowers (as opposed to culinary and medicinal plants) grown both commercially and domestically had increased because of the plant-hunting expeditions of the great botanists. These colourful plants from all the world's temperate zones form the basis of our modern gardens and were being developed and improved by the time Victoria came to the throne. The Victorian posy is a tribute to the colour and variety developed by the early plantsmen.

CHOOSING COLOURS The traditional form of a Victorian posy is rings of flowers arranged around a single central bloom. The finished piece should be light and dainty, with a delicate scent and rich colours. The colour balance should be considered very carefully, since the blooms are arranged tightly against each other. This doesn't mean that you should always play safe in your choice. Rich colours from the opposite sides of the colour wheel look splendid together, and the closeness of the flowers increases their impact.

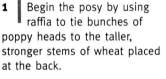

> ### FURTHER INFORMATION
> ☞
> Colour, page **162**
> Glue guns, page **8**
> Wiring, page **114**

HERB AND SPICE POSY

This posy is designed to make a decorative hanging for a kitchen wall, so the stems are arranged to form a flat back. The herbs and spices for this posy are colourful as well as aromatic, although any herbs and spices are suitable. The chilli peppers look very rich with their shiny red skins and although poppies are stretching the herb idea (the seeds are a popular topping for cakes and bread) they make a lovely contrast with the marjoram and rosemary.

1 Begin the posy by using raffia to tie bunches of poppy heads to the taller, stronger stems of wheat placed at the back.

2 Always keep the posy in your left hand (if you are right-handed) and with the right hand twist the raffia firmly round each bunch of herbs as you add them to the design. The raffia holds the bunch quite firmly so you can lay it down on the work-bench to pick up other material as you progress.

3 | To add an interesting touch, add a couple of old terracotta pots on sticks to the front of the design. You just need two pieces of garden cane, about 25cm (10in) long. Push the stick through the hole of the pot, and fix it with a generous blob of glue from a hot glue gun. Add the pots on their sticks at the end as they are not only the trickiest pieces to add but they also need to be at the front of the design.

4 | Position the pots asymmetrically in the design and bind them on very firmly with the raffia. You may find that you have to lay the whole piece down to do this, as the pots are much heavier than the other herbs and spices. Raffia is very strong but has sufficient "give" to allow you to make small adjustments to the finished bunch. Finally, fill the pots up with the beautiful purple flowers of the marjoram, and finish the whole piece off with a large, informal bow of raffia.

DRIED FLOWER VICTORIAN POSY

This is the classic Victorian posy made from dried flowers instead of fresh flowers. The effect of a Victorian posy relies on closely arranging the flower heads in concentric circles around a single central flower. As dried flowers have rigid and sometimes brittle stems, some of the material may need to be wired and taped to make assembly easier.

The choice of flowers is a simple selection of large-headed bright red roses, smaller dark red roses, poppy heads and marjoram. Once a piece like this is made up, it would make a suitable and lasting gift, or it could be used as a bridesmaid's posy.

3 Poppy heads form the next ring. To prevent them moving out of position, it's a good idea to tie the stem with some string or raffia at this stage even though the posy isn't finished.

1 For the centre select three of the most perfect bright red roses, then begin to surround them with darker red roses, working with a firm hand as the roses tend to move out of alignment quite easily.

2 Make the next ring using bright red roses, clasping the stems very firmly and taking care to form a gentle dome shape every time you add another flower.

4 A "collar" of marjoram adds a lacy effect to the posy and contrasts well with the solid globes of poppy heads. Just keep adding stems of the herb until you have achieved the shape you want then finish off with another tie of the raffia.

5 As this is a formal posy a well-matched ribbon completes the piece, which would look pretty standing in a vase or jug.

CLASSIC VICTORIAN POSY

In traditional floristry this posy would be made by wiring and taping individual blooms and binding them to form a compact and formal piece suitable for a bridesmaid or a visiting VIP! However, this posy is simply made from flowers on their natural stems.

2 | Add a thin line of shiny berries after the roses; try to space the material evenly as you add it to the posy, as the finished pieces should have a formal, symmetrical appearance.

1 | Choose your single bloom to go in the middle of the posy. In this case, it is a single anemone stem. Surround the anemone with pink roses in a neat circle. As you build up the posy, keep it in your left hand (if you are right-handed) and, picking up the loose flowers with your right hand, gradually add them to the piece, always

ensuring that the stems lie across each other in the same direction, with the bloom pointing to the top left and the stem pointing down to the right. The posy in the left hand can be turned 45 degrees by passing it from left to right hand and back again, then adding the additional stems.

3 | Follow the berries with a ring of deep violet anemones. These need careful handling as the stems are hollow and prone to snapping. As anemone stems can be very uneven it makes life much easier to select the straightest stems with the most regular size blooms from several bunches. Continue adding the flowers in the same spiralling movement described in step 1.

4 Victorian posies look particularly enchanting if the outer ring is finished off with a collar of leaves. In this case, leaves from *Hedera canariensis* have been used. Thread the heavy wire through the spine of the leaf and then down the ivy stem and finish with florist's tape, so that each leaf can be positioned and curved over in the required position.

5 Secure the completed posy tightly with thin string, and cut off the stems evenly to a suitable length. The stem length should be sufficient for two hands to hold the posy; cut off a little more if it is for a young child. Finish the posy with a complementary ribbon.

WEDDING FLOWERS

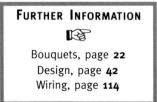

As with everything to do with weddings these days, there are few rules to observe in the choice of flowers. The bride's selection can be as conventional or as off-beat as she wishes; carnations or cauliflowers, the bride must have what she wants.

If you are helping a bride with her wedding flowers, encourage her to look at bride magazines and specialist books, so that she becomes familiar with different types of flowers and designs. Also it's always much easier to talk about bridal flowers when she has chosen her dress and decided on the venue.

CHOOSING FLOWERS AND FOLIAGE Flowers for weddings fall into three parts: bridal flowers including buttonholes and corsages, flowers for the marriage ceremony and flowers for the reception. In most cases the bride will have a theme that she wants to carry through from beginning to end, in other cases she may adapt her choice to suit the setting.

If the wedding is being planned well in advance, check on seasonal availability. If the flowers wanted will not be available, then consider using silk flowers instead. Finally, if you want your flowers to have a really professional look, don't skimp on the foliage. The sorts of foliage that are most useful are rhododendron, berried ivy, trailing ivy, *Viburnum tinus*, laurel, choisya, and in the spring and summer anything with blossom is wonderful and saves on expensive flowers for large pieces.

FURTHER INFORMATION
☞

Bouquets, page **22**
Design, page **42**
Wiring, page **114**

LARGE PEDESTAL ARRANGEMENT

When choosing the flowers for a large piece like this, bear in mind that the display may have to be seen from a distance. You will need large-headed flowers with strong structural shapes; avoid small delicate flowers, and try to include some tall, pointed blooms such as stock, gladioli (much derided but wonderful for this purpose), antirrhinums or delphiniums.

1 Fill a large china cache-pot with soaked foam and anchor the foam securely with florist's tape or wire.

2 Start building up your outline with the different foliage. The foliage will dictate the maximum size of the finished piece; flowers are always placed within this framework. Try to work symmetrically in a gentle fan shape (strict triangles are old fashioned and too formal).

3 Add some foliage to break the horizontal line so that the whole piece flows down as well as up. Keep stepping back from your work as you progress, checking for scale and proportion. This is especially important if you have two matching pieces to make. Once you are satisfied with the overall shape, you can start adding the flowers. Start at the top of the piece, using each variety in turn.

4 Gradually work your way into the centre of the piece, reserving the large open lilies for this purpose. The eye is naturally drawn into the centre of a large piece, so place your stems with great care. Avoid crowding the blooms by allowing enough space around each one. Large open blooms can be cut surprisingly short, trim the stem away gradually until you get the ideal length; don't be tempted to leave all the stems too long in the middle as you will run out of space.

5 The display is now beginning to look balanced and in proportion. The finishing touches come from the white *Euphorbia fulgens* and florist's lilac, cascading elegantly down and out.

PEW END

Arranging flowers at the ends of the pews is an effective and popular way to decorate a church for a wedding. Provided the church has proper pews, and the vicar will allow you to fix floral decorations on to their sides, you should find them fairly straightforward.

1 In this case the pew end arrangement is being made up in situ. Begin by pushing the foam firmly on to the tray, and taping the whole thing to the side of the pew using thin dark green florist's tape. You may have to tape round to the other side as well, so try to do it as neatly as possible. Start building up the shape with the foliage paying particular attention to the outline, but don't cover the front too much and use shorter pieces of foliage for this area.

2 Once you are happy with the outline, start inserting the flowers, working with the longer stems first. The popular lisianthus (*Eustoma grandiflorum*) in white makes an ideal bloom for this purpose with its strong stems and elegant habit. Push the stem in parallel with the pew and as close to the wood as you can.

3 Cut two bright pink antirrhinums very short and place them parallel with the pew to give the piece depth and to fill up the centre.

4 Following through the theme from the bride's own flowers, in this case lilies, place two or three heads of open pale pink oriental lilies near the centre of the piece. As you can see, the foam and tray are becoming well hidden by the flowers.

5 Place the five eye-catching germinis (miniature gerbera) in an asymmetrical line through the arrangement, making sure that they do not project too much as they could be damaged inadvertently by passing guests.

6 A few freesias fanning out from the centre will look dainty and make the church smell delightful.

7 If you have some open roses, they will be perfect to fill in the centre of the pew ends. If you cut them short there will be no danger of wilting and they add a special touch to the design.

FIXINGS

There are several ways to fix the decoration to the pews:

● There is a product specifically designed for the purposes, which hooks over the top of the pew and is secured in position by means of a tight coil of plastic clamped firmly against the wood. The other side contains a round piece of foam enclosed in a plastic "cage" into which you place the flowers. The height is also adjustable. The advantage of this gadget is that you need not use tape or wire to fix the piece, but the disadvantage is that the fixture on the guests' side of the pew end is not very attractive.

● For a country-style wedding a simple bunch of flowers hand-tied with string, then tied over the pew end with a big bow is very pretty. However, if you use this method, the flowers can't be arranged much in advance and have to be hung up shortly before the guests are due to arrive.

● The third method uses a green florist's spray tray with a quarter block of foam taped in place (see left). The advantage to this method is that the tray can be decorated in advance, then taped securely on to the wooden side of the pew, where it will be well concealed by the flowers and foliage.

HALF-CIRCLET HEADDRESS

Nothing looks lovelier than fresh flowers for the bride's hair to match the bouquet she is carrying. However, wiring and assembling a circlet like this requires skill and dexterity, and shouldn't really be undertaken by the inexperienced as the work is time-consuming and intricate and there are few shortcuts.

You need to measure the head of the wearer for the finished size of the piece. Hold the tape measure just above the ear then pass it over the head, following a line that suits the wearer's hair and face, to the other ear. Add another 5cm (2in) for safe measure as it's always easier to shorten than lengthen something. Measure a piece of wire (20 gauge) and cover it with florist's tape. If you are making a full circlet, you will probably have to wire two pieces together. As an alternative to florist's wire and tape, you can use milliner's wire, which is available from the haberdashery section in department stores. This wire can be purchased by the metre and does not need taping.

When choosing the flowers for the circlet, your selection will probably follow the theme of the bouquet. Always consider the scale and choose the daintier flowers for this design. Roses and freesias are always popular, but there are lots of other dainty flowers that can be used as well, and don't forget little pieces of foliage such as ivy, eucalyptus, hebe and berries when in season. A word of warning: early summer growth on foliage, especially ivy, can be very soft and won't last well out of water.

This striking circlet is made from cerise pink anemones, freesia, tuberose and waxflower with little clusters of ivy. It's a good idea to have as much material as possible wired and taped in advance. Arrange all your prepared material on the work-surface in front of you. Add each wired flower in a regular sequence, with clusters of ivy to fill in.

1 To start off the piece, take one flower and hold it in position about 2.5cm (1in) from the end of the main wire, then bind the flower on to the wire with the florist's tape. Don't tape the full length of the silver wire as this will make the completed headdress very heavy. Once the flower is firmly in place, carefully trim the remaining wire with scissors and finish off with the tape. Take care not to leave loose wires in the headdress as they may irritate the scalp.

2 Gradually build up the circlet adding all the flowers and ivy in the same sequence. As this is going to be a deep circlet, place each flower close to the next. You can always make small adjustments to the position of the flowers when the piece is complete.

3 When you are within a few flowers of completing the piece, take the undecorated end of the wire, measure in about 2.5cm (1in), and place and tape the final flower the opposite way, with its loose wire towards the centre, then fill in the rest of circlet with the remaining flowers. The spare wire at each end will be hidden by the wearer's hair and can be used for attaching hairclips. If you are making a full circlet, bend the undecorated ends into a "U" shape, then hook one end through the other to complete the circle.

HAND-TIED WEDDING BOUQUET

The traditional way to make bridal bouquets involves many hours of laborious and time-consuming wiring with difficult and complex assembling. In the last few years a new trend in preparing bridal bouquets has developed; arranging the flowers on their natural stems, to create an informal design with ease of construction. The technique is based on the basic hand-tied construction in which all the stems spiral in the same direction, never allowing them to cross. The main difference is the way you position the flowers, allowing them to flow gracefully down from the hand in a gentle cascade.

Once the bride has chosen her selection of flowers, perhaps with the help of a good flower shop, give the flowers a drink for at least 12 hours before starting. Try to set up a mirror close to your workspace so that you can view the work as you go along. Have ready a piece of string or raffia 60cm (24in) long to bind the finished piece.

Build up the bouquet gradually, starting with the foliage to create the general outline and the overall finished length (see treatment of ivy in step 1) then start adding the flowers and more foliage if necessary, always checking in the mirror for balance. It is best to place the larger focal flowers like the lilies in the centre of the design, with the more "pointed" shapes like the freesia fanning out. Select your material with care, choosing just the right bloom for a particular position, then relax and take your time positioning the flowers just where you want them.

1 Trailing ivy needs a little encouragement to hang in the required direction. The most effective way to do this is to wind a length of wire (20–22 gauge) about half to three-quarters of the way along the stem. Bind the end with florist's tape. You can now bend the ivy stem any way you like but it still looks very natural.

3 | The flower arranger's favourite, eucalyptus, will set off the flowers beautifully. Gently curve the stems in the direction you want. Check your measurements at this stage as

you will now have your overall length and width and, if necessary, make adjustments.

2 | Start to build up a good bunch of foliage in your hand. This gives you a firm base and an outline shape for your flowers. As well as the trailing ivy you can use any attractive foliage from the garden, although it is best to avoid foliage that is too "soft" especially during the early summer when it is growing, as the ends will shrivel after a few hours out of water.

4 | Now insert the flowers, starting with the longer stems, in this case white lisianthius (more correctly *Eustoma grandiflorum*) which is an elegant flower with a natural curve. Arrange the rest of the lisianthius throughout the developing bouquet, using the more open stems nearer the centre of the piece.

5 | This is a good point to put in the lovely pink oriental lilies, and as these are your focal flowers, they should be concentrated around the centre of the design. When you are building up your design, work through the whole bouquet, checking the balance all the time.

6 | Following the shape that is gradually emerging, arrange the tighter buds of freesia to the outside and the open blooms towards the centre. Try to vary their length to add depth to the design.

7 | Astilbe may not be the easiest flower to obtain, but it is well worth the effort as the subtle colour, scent and delicacy is perfect for a wedding bouquet.

8 | Fill in the remaining gaps with a few clusters of dusty pink waxflower. If you do use a filler like waxflower or gypsophila, try to use it sparingly, as too much will detract from the main flowers.

9 | Now check the bouquet in the mirror for balance and to make sure there are no gaps. When you are sure you have finished, you must tie the stems with raffia or string round the point where you have been holding them. (See procedure for hand-tied gift bouquet). Leave a length of about 6 inches, then bind the stems firmly 3 or 4 times and tie the two ends together. The string will be hidden by a lovely satin bow.

WIRES AND WIRING

This technique is used on individual blooms, small clusters of flowers and foliage to create a flexible stem that can be formed to specific shapes. Wiring is used most commonly for bridal work to make buttonholes and corsages, hair pieces and the bride's bouquet. It is also used routinely for extending sections of artificial flowers.

The basic method of wiring applies regardless of application; a bloom is detached from its natural stem, a false stem is then created by pushing a wire through the fleshiest part of the remaining flower, doubling the wire back, twisting it on itself, then sealing the whole false stem with stem tape, which makes an attractive finish and also seals the moisture in the flower. There are countless variations on this technique, and highly experienced florists have their individual methods for all the different types of flowers and foliages, but whichever variation you use, the resulting work should always be as light, delicate and neat as possible, with as little evidence of the mechanics as possible.

> ### FURTHER INFORMATION
> ☞
> Artificial flowers, page **16**

WIRING A ROSE

These steps show you how to wire a rose, which can be made in to a classic buttonhole, to wear to a wedding or the races. Once you have mastered this basic wiring technique, you will be able to build up to more complicated and ambitious pieces as the principles always remain the same.

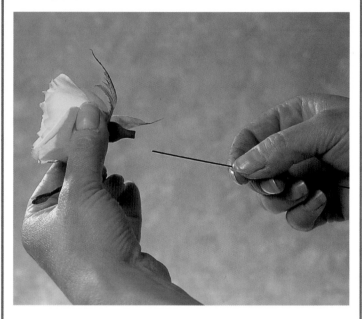

1 Cut the stem of the rose just below the calyx. Holding the flower in one hand, insert an 18cm (7in) length of 0.71mm (22g) wire through the centre of the remaining stem until the wire is secure.

2 Take a 18cm (7in) long piece of silver wire, insert the end in to the calyx at the join with the petals and start winding it round the calyx and stem of the rose making sure the wire is not too slack.

3 | Continue down the stem and around the 0.71mm wire for a few turns to ensure a firm contact between rose and wires.

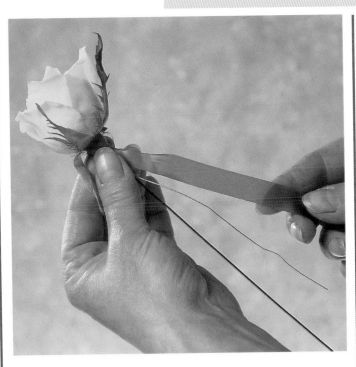

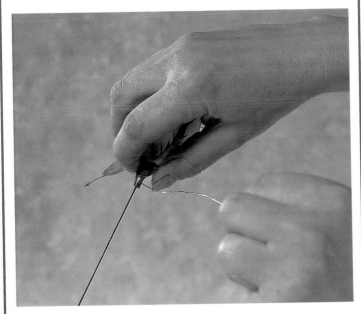

4 | Tape the stem and wires with a green stem tape (there are several types available, so choose the type you are happiest working with) stretching the tape tautly.

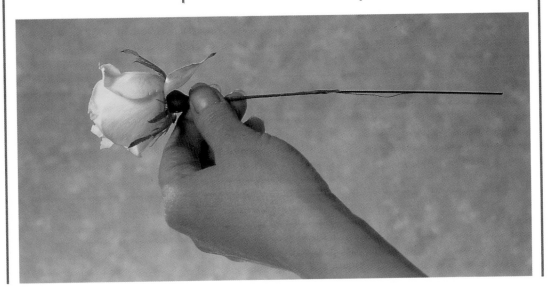

5 | If you are making a buttonhole, cut through the wire leaving about 8cm (3in) then continue the tape to the end, making sure the sharp end of the wire is well covered. However, if the rose is going in to a larger piece, tape down the stem for about 5cm (2in) leaving the wire uncut.

WIRING A FREESIA BUD

Although the buds of freesias are delicate and difficult to handle, they are ideal for corsages and hair pieces, and last surprisingly well. To wire freesia buds, you will need to use the lightest gauge rose wire; however you can use the whole stem of freesia, basically following the same technique as the rose.

1 | Detach an open bud from a stem of freesia, removing all the stem, then using the lightest silver wire, gently pierce the flower about one third from the base taking great care not to tear the fragile petals.

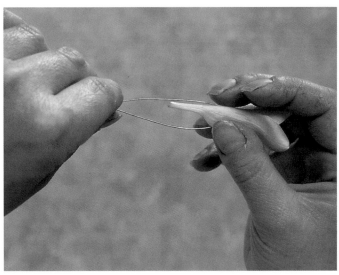

2 | Push the silver wire through to the other side of the flower and double back.

3 | Wind one end of the wire round the flower base and along the other end of the wire to form a "single leg mount". It is easy to crush the delicate buds, so the lightest of touches is required for this procedure.

4 | Start your stem tape above the point where the wire enters the bud to make sure that all the moisture is retained within the flower.

5 | Continue taping down the stem for about 5cm (2in), gently stretching the tape as you work to form a seal.

ADAPTING SILK FLOWERS AND FOLIAGE

A whole stem of flowers or leaves may be more than you need for a particular arrangement. With this technique you can break up the stem into smaller units by cutting up sections and wiring the portions, either on to a long wire to go in an arrangement or on short wires for bridal work.

1 Using a pair of strong scissors or wire cutters cut the tough stems of variegated ivy in to smaller clusters, retaining as much of the stem as possible.

2 Take a wire that is strong enough to support the head, and with it make a single leg mount.

3 Tape over the whole stem and the wire extension.

If you are embarking on a project in which wiring is required, it is important to bear these two points in mind:
• When selecting flowers that are suitable for wiring, consider the size and shape of the blooms, and also their lasting qualities, for instance roses and freesia are always a popular choice as are classics like orchids and stephanotis for brides' bouquets. In principle the fleshier the flower, the better it will last.
• Always choose the right gauge and length of wire for the type of bloom and position in the piece. It should be as light as possible at the same time strong enough to support the head of the flower.
Have ready a good selection of wire gauges and lengths (including silver wires), reel wire, stem tape and strong sharp scissors, and if necessary, wire cutters.

Wreaths

Traditionally used as floral tributes at funerals or as decorations for celebrating Advent and Christmas, wreaths can be made for so many different occasions and places in the home you hardly need an excuse to make one.

Here are a few themed ideas you may like to try: a Christening or nursery wreath; a wreath for a new kitchen, using old kitchen implements as well as dried herbs, bags of bouquet garni and bulbs of garlic; a musical wreath, using scrolls of sheet music and toy instruments; a child's wreath using small rag dolls holding hands round the ring.

BASIC WREATHS The basic wreath frame comes in three forms: foam-filled rings with a solid plastic base for soaking and using with fresh flowers and greenery (they can be used unsoaked for dried flowers or it is possible to buy foam for dry use), copper wire frames which are filled with moss to make a base for attaching the finishing materials; or twig rings, which can be bought at shops selling dried flowers. You can of course make a wreath yourself from lengths of bendy stem such as clematis or vine, which you twine round and round until the ring shape is formed. If it is a bit loose, just bind it with string or raffia to strengthen.

> **FURTHER INFORMATION**
> ☞
> Materials, page **8**

CHRISTENING WREATH

Why not make something a bit different for a new godchild? This unusual wreath can be hung on the nursery wall and will be a lasting reminder of a special event in the child's life. The materials for this piece came from various sources, both old and new, including an antique ivory and silver teething ring, a pair of baby socks, hand-painted letters and a piece of nursery fabric.

1 | The base for the wreath is a ready-made willow ring available from florists or basket shops. Start by tying the fabric and arranging it in a big bow, then add the letters to make the child's name fixing them with a hot glue gun; tie the teething ring in place with raffia.

2 | Glue the soft rag clown to the frame to balance the wooden letters. The design is beginning to take shape now.

3 It is best to stitch the socks together before gluing them in place. Write your message on the gift tag and glue or tie on to the wreath.

4 Dried rose heads make a pretty finishing touch to this delightful and original gift. Just apply some hot glue to the cut-off stem and push on to the wreath frame.

CHRISTMAS WREATH

A traditional evergreen wreath hung on the front door is very welcoming at Christmas. You can use any greenery for the base: trimmings from your Christmas tree, ivy, or luxurious "blue" pine shown here. To decorate the wreath you can add whatever you have to hand. Keep to a limited colour scheme or choose a theme such as food, including cinnamon sticks, gold-sprayed nuts and slices of preserved orange. You can also add a few favourite Christmas tree decorations. Finish with a generous bow to hang up your wreath and disguise the fixing.

A smaller wreath makes a good centrepiece for a dinner table. Choose one to suit the size of your table without taking up too much valuable space. If you include candles, be careful not to let them burn down to the greenery.

1 | Using a copper wire frame, gradually cover it with tight "sausages" of moss, working round the ring, and securing the "sausages" by firmly winding the reel wire over the moss and frame, until all the ring is filled with moss.

2 | The covering to this wreath is "blue" pine, which is a wonderful evergreen that stays fresh for weeks and doesn't lose its needles. Bunch together 2–3 small pieces of pine, fanning them slightly, then attach them to the moss base by looping reel wire round the stems. Keep overlapping the pine pieces, continuing until the whole frame is covered. The reel wire will be hidden by the overlapping pieces of pine. Knot the end of the wire securely like a piece of thread. Finally, make a good strong hanger with several loops of wire at the top of the wreath. The loops should be large enough to hook over a front door knob.

3 | Now the wreath is ready to be decorated. Bind several cinnamon sticks together with raffia, then thread stub wire through and double it back, push into the pine and moss base, and secure wires firmly at the back.

6 | Use a short piece of wire to make a loop for hanging. Twist the ends together as shown.

4 | Wire on several slices of preserved dried orange in the same way, fanning out two or three slices, then pushing the wire through the flesh, doubling it back and pushing it into the pine and moss base to secure the cluster.

5 | Finish decorating the wreath with gold-sprayed lotus pods, mixed nuts in their shells (these can be glued on with a hot glue gun if you prefer) and gold-threaded sinamay ribbon.

KITCHEN WREATH

The base of this wreath is a ready-made twiggy ring, which is fairly readily available from garden centres and florists. If you have trouble buying one, they are easily made in the autumn and winter from lengths of clematis or Russian vine, twined round and round until a firm wreath is formed. Just tuck the last piece of stem into the wreath to finish it off.

2 | Now glue two pieces of driftwood in position across the wreath. Driftwood has a beautiful natural rhythm, and lovely bleached finish; it is nature's sculpture and adds a special quality to this sort of unusual composition.

1 | To liven up the composition, it can be fun to introduce a piece of fabric. You will need about a metre (yard) of cloth. Red gingham has been used in this piece, but it would be equally successful with butter muslin or blue gingham or a piece of fabric already used in curtains or blinds in your kitchen. Roll the fabric on the bias into a sausage shape, wind it round the ring, and secure it in several places with raffia bows.

3 | Now glue or tie on freeze-dried whole oranges and freeze-dried sliced oranges.

4 | Now glue on the other chosen materials such as dried chilli peppers, clusters of cinnamon sticks and dried corn-on-the-cob.

5 | To complete the kitchen theme, add accessories such as an old butter pat and a wooden fork, which cross the wreath under the driftwood. Add a small blob of glue where they come in contact with the wreath to secure them in place. Any old wooden kitchen utensils can be used successfully in a piece like this, and they can be picked up reasonably cheaply in junk shops.

THEMES

Flower arranging is one of the world's oldest crafts. In ancient cultures flowers were used to decorate places of worship, then gradually they were introduced to the home on special occasions. Nowadays flowers are an important part of all our lives, giving the flower arranger ample opportunity to produce creative arrangements to enhance every room.

OCCASIONS

No celebration would be complete without the special touch that flowers bring to an occasion whatever the time of year. Inspiration and ingenuity can make up for even the most limited budgets; lovely flowers need not cost the earth if you choose a seasonal selection with lots of interesting foliage.

If you are making the floral decorations for a particular occasion, try to find out if there's a theme, and work around that. The most obvious themes are seasonal and religious ones, such as Christmas, Easter and harvest festivals, which have a very strong influence on colour and materials. Christenings, first communions, marriages and funerals also call for floral decorations. Birthdays, wedding anniversaries and special parties are also fun to commemorate with flowers.

▲ Iron candelabras have become very popular in the last few years and are easy to decorate. Cover the whole structure with moss and decorate just with white flowers to make a very striking festive decoration.

◀ This iron candle holder is on a smaller scale, perfect for dressing an intimate dinner party table. The candle holder is surrounded by an arrangement of evergreens, tulips, roses and bright red holly berries.

CHRISTMAS

In the Northern hemisphere the beginning of the winter season is an absolute gift to the creative flower designer. There is an abundance of natural foliages, mosses and berries, and the shops are full of excellent ribbons, as well as traditional and modern decorations that can be used to make festive pieces.

In the Southern hemisphere, a combination of red flowers, cool foliage, ribbons and baubles will give a festive touch that suits the summer weather.

▲ Dating back to the pre-Christian pagan winter festival, this variation on a "kissing bough" is a most attractive decoration, using large, medium and small wire wreath frames, covered in lasting evergreens and decorated with apples and candles. The whole piece is hung by a ribbon from the ceiling.

◄ There is no need to confine decorations to the more usual places like tables and mantelpieces. A window sill is brightened up by seasonal foliages and colours and lit candles which reflect romantically against the window pane.

▶ Greet your guests in the festive spirit with a door wreath. Wherever you live, front doors hung with wreaths make a joyful sight for visitors and passers-by.

◀ The appeal of this vase arrangement is its simplicity – fresh green evergreens, combined with bright red roses, and dotted with festive bows, walnuts and pine cones. The cones, nuts and bows are attached to long heavy gauge wires and pushed into the arrangement.

HARVEST FESTIVAL

Giving thanks for the blessings of the season goes back centuries. Most cultures and religions celebrate the gathering of the harvest in some way, and it is a great opportunity to make decorative use of fruit, vegetables, dried wheat and flowers, knotted breads and the colourful flowers, leaves and berries of late summer and early autumn. As well as the produce in the harvest festival service, the place of worship itself is decorated with fruit and flowers which represent various aspects of the gathering of crops and the giving of thanks for earth's abundance. In the Jewish religion, a temporary structure is built in the garden, decorated with fruits, sheaves of wheat, large loaves of bread, in which all family meals are eaten during the festival.

► Van Gogh immortalized sunflowers in his paintings, and they have been grown in Mediterranean countries for centuries as an important source of oil and seed. Throughout the summer acres of brilliant yellow and black daisy heads brighten the fields of France.

► This group of baskets and arrangements shows just a small selection of the vast range of dried flowers available these days. The flowers are cut and hung to dry during the long summer days when they are at their best. Most will be ready for purchasing by the end of the summer.

▲ | Why not make a harvest festival wreath? Decorate a ready-made willow wreath with a big raffia bow and seasonal accessories.

▼ | For a really luxurious and seasonal display, this mantel decoration would be difficult to surpass. A piece like this would look good all through the winter, and could be slightly modified for the Christmas season.

SPRING

Spring flowers seem to arrive earlier and earlier in our flower shops each year and hold a promise that is unmatched by any other season. From the first snowdrops to the bright, almost garish tulips of late spring, every week brings its own treasures. Bulbs, especially narcissi, are most associated with spring, but there is a wealth of wonderful early flowering shrubs, particularly in the viburnum family, which are very beautiful and heavily scented.

The arrival of spring has always been a reason for celebration and, from pre-Christian times, most major religions have some sort of spring festival. In the northern hemisphere, the holidays of Good Friday and Easter Sunday are the most important in the Christian calendar, particularly as they mark the end of a period of fasting and austerity. During Lent the church is unadorned by flowers until Easter Sunday, when it is transformed by white lilies and yellow daffodils.

▶ In Holland and Germany, Easter trees are very popular. A selected tree branch is hung with a variety of special Easter ornaments. This was the inspiration behind this modern arrangement, which teams a decorated branch with the other Easter traditional materials of yellow flowers and candles.

▶ This vase is filled with an abundant display of typical spring flowers, such as tulips, freesias, ranunculuses, scented genista, roses and lots of interesting foliage.

◀ You could decorate the Easter Sunday lunch table with a really special celebration piece like this. The group of four candles placed close together give the arrangement impact and add a special atmosphere.

FLOWERS IN A RELIGIOUS SETTING

Flowers play an important part in many religious ceremonies. For example in Hindu weddings both the bride and groom wear garlands of flowers and during the ceremony they are sprinkled with rose petals. The lotus or water lily is the symbolic flower of Hindu India, and in religious art, deities are depicted sitting on a multi-petalled lotus throne. Also in the East, entrances to Buddhist shrines are decorated with bowls of lotus flowers.

In the West, the Celtic Druids of Ancient Britain and northern France used mistletoe in their midwinter solstice festival (surprisingly, it was also used in the summer solstice festival), a custom that still survives in traditional Christmas decorations today both as a symbol of luck and fertility and to denote a safe welcome within. Flowers are well represented in mythology, for example, red anemones symbolize Adonis's spilt blood.

▲ | The Jewish festival, the Feast of Chanukah, which usually coincides with Christmas, is also known as the Festival of Lights, in which each of the candles in the seven-branched menorah are lit in turn every day for a week.

► | A spectacular piece designed to go on the altar in the shape of a cross, which would look most appropriate at Easter, when the flowers appear again after their absence during Lent.

Flowers are an important and traditional feature of funerals for many religions. This magnificent wreath has been constructed with enormous love and attention to detail; it would make a most appropriate and touching tribute.

This marble alcove has been filled with a lovely flowing display of flowers mounted on a candle holder, with a big church candle in the top.

SPECIAL DAYS

There are many days during the year when celebrating with flowers is appropriate, for instance: birthdays, anniversaries, feast days, Mother's Day, the birth of a baby, jubilee celebrations and so on. The choice of flowers can be as simple or as grand as is fitting, and should reflect both the occasion and the recipient's own taste. Sometimes the occasion is made more special by a surprise delivery of a bouquet, so try to plan this in advance with your florist, who will be able to advise you about suitable flowers for the day.

In recent years, there has been a development in non-traditional gift days, for instance Father's day and Grandparents' day, and although these are modern marketing tactics, nevertheless flowers are always greatly appreciated.

▶ A basket crammed with snowdrops would make the most adorable present for the birth of a winter baby.

◀ A basket filled with flowers ranging from soft pink to bright cerise includes freesias for their scent and roses to add a touch of luxury. The handle of the basket has been decorated with ribbons.

▼ | A large candlestick holding a large church candle, decorated round the outside with flowers, is a traditional floral decoration for Greek Orthodox weddings and christenings.

▲ | A bouquet made up of a selection of dried flowers would make a most appropriate present for Mother's Day. They could then be put straight in a vase or arranged in a basket.

WEDDINGS

Of all special occasions, weddings would not be complete without flowers for the bride, the wedding guests, the place where the ceremony takes place, and the reception.

Providing flowers for a wedding requires a lot of planning, particularly as they cannot be made up much in advance. If you are planning to do the flowers for a large wedding try to make up a schedule beforehand so that you know exactly what you are doing and when, and if you have recruited some help, your helpers will know exactly what is required of them as well.

◀ Decorating the pews in a church is a most effective floral treatment and in this particular case a little unusual as the pew is not decorated, as is customary, on the aisle side but inside the pew, allowing the flowers to drape gracefully round each side.

▼ The elaborate carving in the side chapel of this very grand church needs to be balanced with a strong colour scheme. The pink and blue pick up the colours in the marble, and the red makes a striking contrast.

◀ Lots of green and white make a beautiful combination for this column decoration or plaque. Constructing a piece like this can be a little tricky, but well worth the effort for this result.

INSPIRATIONS

From earliest times, flowers in all their forms have inspired the work of artists and designers. In turn, flower arrangers are often inspired by works of art, seeking to recreate an arrangement from a painting, or to make an arrangement that looks like a still life.

Contemporary floral artists and designers often turn to the past for their own sources. Seventeenth-century Flemish and Dutch still-life paintings, themselves inspired by the introduction of new flowers from the East, are wonderful to recreate with their opulent cascade of strong colours and shapes.

The East is a constant source of interest, both for its exotic flowers, plants and fruit and also for its art and artefacts which feature flowers in realistic and stylized forms. Flower design as art reaches its apotheosis in Japan, where flower arranging to ancient and formal principles is taught and practised as a true art form.

▲ This show piece has been created as a Japanese tableau, and includes materials, such as bamboo, which are associated with Japan. Woven grass forms the background to the flowers.

▲ In this setting a fine
balance is held between
the clashing patterns and
shapes by careful use of
colour. The flowery chintz
background cloths are
balanced by the cool blue of
the china and the simple
yellow and white colour
scheme for the flowers and
fruit.

ART

The beauty of nature, and flowers in particular, has been the subject of paintings for centuries. Originally flowers were used for purely symbolic reasons, for instance the *Lilium candidum* held by the Virgin Mary in the wonderful Fra Angelico frescoes. From the seventeenth century onwards the paintings of Northern Europe became more purely decorative, with an increase in paintings depicting nature realistically for its own sake.

◀ The flowers are arranged on a flat surface to form a piece of decorative artwork. The inspiration for the pattern comes from the combination of shapes and colours of the flowers.

▶ This informal bowl of garden flowers could have been the subject for a painting by Monet or Cézanne.

▲ | Like a painting by Rembrandt the interest of this composition comes from the dramatic use of light and shade. The pewter and black china containers reflect light and contrast with the rich reds and coppers of the flowers, fruit and foreground cloth.

▼ | A raid on the rose garden has produced a lovely composition of roses at their various stages from bud to full blown. It gives you an opportunity to admire the wonderful structure of the petals within a rose head.

IKEBANA

Japanese flower arranging, known as ikebana, is taught throughout the world. It has its foundations in Zen Buddhism, with the three main elements representing heaven, earth and man. This is a very different approach to flower arranging in the European manner, where abundance and decorative values predominate.

In Japan everyone is taught the fundamentals of this highly skilled art form, as it is part of their cultural heritage. The materials used are seasonal leaves, flowers and branches placed in traditional containers usually made from natural glazed pottery. The simplicity of the design allows the observer to appreciate the full beauty of each element. If a shallow container is used the materials need to be anchored on a metal "pincushion".

In ikebana the depiction of nature's beauty is always counterbalanced with a reminder of the briefness and harshness of life by the inclusion of, for example, a piece of decaying matter or a rough stone to contrast with a perfect bloom.

▲ In this competition piece the designer contrasts the lightness of heaven with the solid abundance of earth – the delicate willow arching over the dense undergrowth, lightened by a sweeping line of pink nerines.

▼ If ikebana aims for simplicity of expression, then this piece has surely achieved it. With a tight control over the vertical and horizontal lines, the designer has made the sparse materials come to life in a work of art.

▶ This Dutch interpretation of the Japanese style follows the same principles of simplicity and balance, creating a graceful asymmetrical piece.

◀ The designer of this piece has allowed the wayward line of the forsythia to cut across the carefully controlled vertical lines of the rest of the piece.

SIMPLICITY

In the spring nothing could be more lovely than a bunch of daffodils in a jug. From their unpromising start as thin stems they open to perfect yellow trumpets, revealing the promise of returning spring. Summer simplicity is an old cut-glass bowl overflowing with mixed roses; as the petals fall gently round the bowl on to the table they enhance the effect.

In a book about techniques, the emphasis is usually on careful and clever construction and design; in this section the true beauty of the flowers is allowed to speak for itself. Whatever the flower, the success of the display is enhanced by the right container. It's worth building up a collection of shapes, from old jugs found in junk shops to simple modern glass vases, so that you always have just the right container for your flowers.

▲ | This is a traditional art basket from Japan, designed to take a simple bloom. It would probably sit in an alcove in the home.

▶ | This amaryllis planted in an old terracotta pot makes a very attractive display. Cover the soil with moss and wind a piece of contorted willow round the long hollow stems of the plant to keep them upright.

◀ The ultimate in minimalism – a single bloom in a plain glass vase sitting on the edge of a black lacquered trestle table.

▶ Narcissi are plentiful in spring and you can afford to be extravagant with them. The simple addition of fresh white and green foliage is all that is needed.

COMBINATIONS

**As well as the foliage and container, flowers are
often combined with other materials, either as part of
a theme or to produce an original design by
extending the scope of the traditional materials
available to the flower designer.**

The possibilities are endless, starting with the more usual ribbons
and bows, to fruit and vegetables, candles, terracotta, shells, fungi,
ropes and fabrics.

      Flowers may be combined or attached to the most unlikely
objects if they can be introduced in an unself-conscious manner. If
the whole effect is balanced, it will work effortlessly. In Holland, for
example, any occasion is an excuse to introduce flowers, and the
Dutch will decorate any object that is likely to be the centre of
attention. Car bonnets, for instance, are always decorated with large
floral displays for a wedding.

▲ A highly imaginative
combination of plants,
ribbons, gold bauble, and
small pine cones is unified by
a metal thread to make an
original Christmas arrangement.

◀ The rich colours of the anemones are combined with other flowers within the same colour range and set off with bright pink candles.

FRUIT AND VEGETABLES

The introduction of fruit and vegetables into flower designs can give the arranger the opportunity to create exciting and unusual displays. We generally take fruit and vegetables very much for granted, but their colours and textures can be just as vibrant or as subtle as flowers; and not just their skins – the flesh of the fruit can be as attractive to look at as to eat.

The obvious time for combining fruit, vegetables and flowers is at harvest festival, when we have an opportunity to celebrate the season of "mellow fruitfulness", but other times of the year yield equally rich crops. With a bit of ingenuity many of the fruits of midsummer can be combined –

with flowers. Strawberries, for instance, provided they aren't too ripe can be wired into arrangements, and fresh cherries with their rich colours varying from scarlet and yellow to deep burgundy would enhance any design, even if they were just scattered around the base of a simple table posy.

But it is vegetables which have the most possibilities, with their wonderful shapes and textures. For example shiny purple aubergines, deep green broccoli and all the different shapes of squash which are now available. Exploring the local supermarket or greengrocer can pay dividends for inspiration, and as a bonus, they tend to be light on the pocket!

▲ Terracotta always complements flowers beautifully, and seems to go with all colours and varieties. The ridge in the pot adds texture to the combination.

◀ The rich green and red colour scheme of this tightly packed basket makes its impact with the contrasting textures of the autumn fruits and flowers.

A "Byzantine pyramid" of dried flowers has a line of dried pomegranates spiralling through it.

COMBINING WITH CANDLES

In the last few years the choice of candles and candle holders has widened enormously, with delicious scented candles, slow-burning church candles, night lights and floating candles, and special candlesticks and candelabra that are designed for holding flowers as well as candles.

Candles are always traditional at Christmas, on their own, in table arrangements or to decorate the mantelpiece but why restrict their use to that festival when they can add so much to any celebration, from a large wedding reception to an intimate dinner party. Candlelight casts a flattering glow on guests and flowers and as you will see from the following examples, candles and flowers are a marriage made in heaven.

▶ Candle wax dripping down the candlestick adds a touch of the baroque to this rich tapestry of fruit, flowers and nuts and the light makes the lilies glow like gold.

▶ | This scene creates a magical atmosphere of crisp winter mornings with trees covered in hoarfrost. The exuberant decoration around the window is delicately lit by the candles below.

▲ | A modern parallel Christmas arrangement combining a terracotta bowl with evergreen foliage, bark and two types of candles; round white ones stepping up through the design with two red ones at the top.

COMBINING WITH NATURAL MATERIALS

Extending your range by including natural non-flower materials is to the serious flower arranger what a full palette of colours is to a painter who has only ever used primary colours. It gives you the opportunity to introduce the unexpected into a piece and to enhance certain aspects of the design by creating a theme or atmosphere.

Favourite materials to use are shells, coral, moss, driftwood, twigs, branches, roots, fabric, pine cones, dried fungi and mushrooms. The possibilities are endless and can often be the inspiration for an idea. For instance a wonderful piece of bleached driftwood has the most wonderful sculptural quality and natural movement and can be used in many different contexts. Why not start building up a collection of materials that appeal to you; many cost very little and with a bit of imagination you can extend your fresh or dried flowers.

▲ This arrangement is a study in textures, with strong contrasts between spiky, dried flowers and softly draped fabrics. The colour balance is carefully controlled.

▲ This piece is simplicity itself. A mass of daffodils set on a wonderful piece of tree trunk with pieces of ivy to fill in any gaps.

▶ An abstract piece with dramatic lighting giving an almost stormy effect. The design combines wild grasses with deep red lilies and a variety of pods and dried vegetation.

◀ It's not just the huge basket full of bright sunflowers that appeals in this picture but the whole setting, from the texture of the wall, to the fruit on the shelf.

ACCESSORIES

The idea of building a design around an object or theme is very popular among flower arranging art groups. They may be asked, for example, to provide a floral interpretation of an important moment in history. The theme or object is really just a trigger to the creative process. If you have selected one or two appropriate pieces that express the particular theme, you may intend to build them into your design, blending them with the flowers in a seamless fashion, alternatively you may want to build your design directly on to the structure. Whichever method you choose it's important to allow the design to express the theme symbolically without a need for verbal explanations.

▶ │ This is a completely free-style piece, combining seemingly unrelated objects such as black glass balls, a lush cascade of wide ribbon, cinnamon sticks and a fold of very shiny, bright pink PVC.

▲ | The main theme for this
piece comes from the
orange flavoured tea,
introducing the box and the
loose sachets in to the design
and picking up the colour with
the flowers and candles.

▶ | A wonderful old hobby
horse on wheels has
been decorated with an
exuberant spray of intensely
bright clashing colours giving it
a fairground quality.

FLOWERS IN INTERIORS

Cut flowers are a simple pleasure but the full beauty of an arrangement of flowers will never be realized if the setting is not taken into consideration. In a well-designed interior all the elements of colour, texture, space, form, light and shade come together in harmony; the flowers should fall into that pattern effortlessly, enhancing rather than competing with the surroundings.

Following the same principles as an interior designer selecting materials, choose your flowers so that their colour, shape and texture will blend with the room's furnishings. If the room is a modern, minimalist interior a few simple stems of one type of flower often looks more effective than a big mixed bunch. Conversely, a mixture of simple garden flowers and herbs in a pretty Victorian jug placed on a cottage windowsill completes the setting.

Once you have selected the flowers you need to choose the container. There are so many different types available – galvanized florist's buckets, terracotta pots, hand-painted vases and jugs, baskets and a wide selection of glassware – to suit any setting.

▲ Lilies, normally associated with formal occasions, are arranged in a basket and look just right in this cottage setting.

▲ In complete contrast this sweeping double staircase is on a grand and formal scale. The large oriental-style vase is filled with a permanent display of dried and artificial materials.

STYLE

Having selected the flowers and the container, the next step is to arrange the flowers in a style to harmonize with the setting. The serious flower arranger should be a master of versatility. And like a serious cook who collects recipes, it is a good idea to start a collection of inspiring magazine pictures showing flowers in particular settings for future reference.

Try to use other materials that help to create the right "look" for the space, for instance twigs and contorted willow for modern settings or a good selection of cut foliages from the shrubbery for a country house.

Once you feel confident that all your materials are just right it's always better to try to assemble the arrangement in its final position, however do cover any delicate surfaces and floors with protective sheets.

▲ | This classic triangle-shaped arrangement for autumn combines grapes, cones and pheasant feathers with golden flowers and foliage. Bunches of artificial grapes are ideal for flower arranging and can look very realistic.

▼ | A huge piece of laburnum blossom in a tall lily vase is perfect in this Japanese-inspired setting.

▼ An exciting arrangement made in the European style with sunflowers, bulrushes and sprays of asparagus "sprengeri" fern, which would look completely at home in a modern setting.

▲ The small lily-like trumpets of alstroemeria come in a range of colours from cream to pink, orange and red. They last well in water and look good simply spiralled in a glass vase.

USING COLOUR

When you are deciding on your choice of flowers for a particular setting, colour will probably be your first consideration. In some interiors you may not have any constraints, so the choice will depend on the occasion and season. However in a room with strong patterns it's best to pick up the two or three predominant colours from the main fabric or wallpaper.

As flowers themselves are often the inspiration for fabric, wallpaper, paintings and even ceramics, it can be fun to match a strongly graphic design with the same in fresh flowers if they are available. Pick up one or two of the other colours from the pattern and interpret the design in your own way.

▶ | Flowers seem to be appearing more and more in offices. This soft pink and green posy arrangement would relax any overstressed executive.

▲ | This colourful vase has a strong Mediterranean feel, enhanced by the yellow painted brickwork and blue check tablecloth. The primary colours are skilfully arranged to a fine balance.

▲ The orange flowers pick up the colour of the trimmings on the curtains, cushions and tiebacks in a room with a tricky colour scheme.

◀ Blue and yellow are on opposite sides of the colour wheel and are known as complementary contrasts. The blue background intensifies the yellow of the sunflowers.

POSITIONING FLOWER ARRANGEMENTS

No matter how well you have arranged your flowers, if they are in the wrong position all your hard work will be for nothing. The arrangement should be large enough to be seen yet small enough to fill the space available.

If you are making flowers for a dinner table remember to keep the finished arrangement low enough for the guests to be able to see each other easily and to leave enough space for cutlery and accessories.

If you are decorating a large room, for instance a church or a conference room, it's a good idea to choose bold shapes like lilies and gerberas and tall flowers like gladioli and delphiniums. Although they can be expensive a few of the right type of flower can go a long way.

▶ | The innovative grouping of materials in this ultra-modern tripod arrangement increases its three-dimensional quality; it would make a stunning display for an office reception or a hotel lobby.

The effect of this sleek, uncluttered cream and white dining and living room is softened by a bowl of dainty pink roses.

Most modern offices are decorated in impersonal colour schemes of black, white and grey. To counteract this blandness tubs of tropical plants and bowls of fresh flowers on the tables help to soften the stark effect.

FLOWERS TO WEAR

The most obvious occasion for carrying flowers is a wedding, of course, but there are other occasions when you can wear a simple buttonhole or a flower-trimmed hat.

Wearing or carrying flowers has a long tradition – nosegays were popular among ladies of court in Elizabethan times. The tight posy of scented herbs was held close to the nose when walking through evil smelling streets, and until quite recently a gentleman was never seen without a fresh flower buttonhole. Oscar Wilde, by all accounts a dandy, always sported a green carnation buttonhole.

Flowers are everywhere at weddings. As well as the bride's bouquet, there are posies or baskets of flowers for the bridesmaids to carry. For the bride and bridesmaid's hair there are full flower rings, Alice band style half-circlets and decorated combs to choose from. The groom and best man may wear buttonholes and the bridal party corsages or hats decorated with flowers.

▲ A corsage should be as light as possible so as not to damage delicate fabrics. This corsage has been beautifully assembled from interesting materials.

An elegant design of great simplicity in a modern style. Purple-blues and white roses at the centre are surrounded by large leaves and delicate sprays of grass and fern.

CORSAGES AND BUTTONHOLES

Buttonholes are usually worn at weddings by the groom and immediate wedding party. They can also be spotted at summer race meetings. Carnations are always popular, and the big question is whether or not they should be finished with fern! Roses have gained popularity in recent years and the humble cornflower makes a simple variation on the buttonhole theme.

Corsages are usually worn by the mothers of the bride and groom and are popular at proms and other formal dances. The flowers need to be skilfully assembled on fine silver wires in the lightest possible way so that the finished piece does not pull the fabric of the outfit.

▶ | Freesias are always a favourite for corsages as they have such a delightful scent. They also keep very well when wired, which is an important consideration during hot weather.

▲ | Pink roses never lose their popularity, and here they are skilfully combined with astilbe and small pieces of greenery including ivy leaves.

▶ This is an unusual way to use lily of the valley, with ornamental grass and galax leaves. The leaves are formed into tight scrolls in the centre of the piece and as part of the background.

▼ Another white corsage, but this time the feature flower is the unusual and delicately scented "Amazon lily" (Eucharis grandiflora).

▼ A corsage may be small, but it offers the designer an opportunity to experiment with colour and texture. A single amaryllis bloom is combined with other red flowers and finished with a trail of Spanish moss.

BOUQUETS

The bouquet flowers are probably the most important flowers of the wedding day. Time should be spent with the bride suggesting and selecting the most appropriate flowers, colours and design. She will need to be reassured that the final design will be just the right shape and size to suit her height and shape and the design of the dress.

There are several methods of constructing a bouquet. 1) The traditional wired method where flowers are cut from their natural stems and taped on to long wires before assembling. This is a highly skilled, lengthy and therefore expensive method. 2) Flowers arranged in a foam-filled cone. The flowers are retained on their natural stems and pushed into soaked foam. This is a simpler and quicker way to achieve a traditional bouquet. 3) A hand-tied bouquet, in which the natural stems are arranged in the flower arranger's hand to produce a very natural and informal design that has recently been very popular.

◀ A finished hand-tied bouquet sitting in a vase awaiting presentation to the bride. This is an unusual design in that the emphasis is upwards as opposed to the usual downwards flow.

▲ This would make a lovely bouquet for a spring wedding, with the golden yellow freesias and ranunculus and trails of genista.

▼ | By contrast a subtle piece in purple and lilac with silvery eucalyptus leaves. The leaves have been stripped off the stems and reassembled in overlapping discs to form long trails.

◀ | This bright red modern design would appeal to a bride who likes to make a fashion statement. The flowers have been assembled with great skill and the different elements balance perfectly.

◀ | A famous example of the traditional wired "shower" bouquet, including "pipped" stephanotis buds, orchids and lily of the valley. In fact, this bouquet was made for the wedding of the Princess of Wales.

HATS AND HEADDRESSES

A new hat can be expensive, so instead why not consider decorating an old one with fresh flowers? You can simply pin the flowers straight on to the brim or arrange them in a more elaborate way, like a corsage, which will make the piece lighter and longer lasting.

Flowers for the hair can be as simple or elaborate as the outfits and occasion demand. The bride may wish to have a delicate "tiara" of flowers in the front of her veil, or a large coronet of sumptuous blooms sitting below the hairline. Young flowergirls look enchanting with circles of flowers in their hair, while older bridesmaids may prefer decorated combs. The construction of all hair pieces is elaborate and time-consuming, particularly if there are several bridesmaids. Each flower has to be wired and then taped on to a covered wire and as yet there are no short cuts. So a word of warning, if you have agreed to undertake this work – leave yourself enough time.

▲ Large silk flowers in delicate shades of mauve and pink add pretty detailing and a soft, feminine touch to a hat. Choose the largest blossoms for the centre focal point, wiring layers of smaller frilly-edged flowers round the brim.

◄ An inexpensive bamboo hat is transformed into a stylish accessory with the addition of feathers and an assortment of dried yellow flowers in natural wheat, yellow and coppery orange colours.

◀ A romantic circlet of "The Fairy" spray roses. This is an excellent garden rose that is ideal for cutting.

▶ An easy way to embellish a simple straw hat is to pin or sew a posy of dried flowers to a ribbon tied round the hat. Here, deep purple flower heads provide eye-catching interest with sprays of white flowers and hare's tail grass added for contrast and highlights.

INDEX

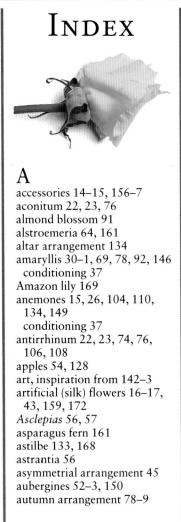

CREDITS

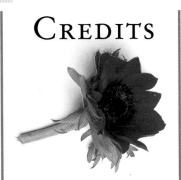

The author would like to thank Katharine Cole, Giovana Ferrari, Suzie Smith, and all the staff at Pot Pourri for their help with the book. She would also like to thank Let Them Eat Cake, 10 Barley Mow Passage, London W4 4PH for supplying the cake on pages 82–3.

Quarto would like to thank the following individuals and agencies for supplying photographs and for permission to reproduce copyright material. While every effort has been made to trace and acknowledge all copyright holders, we would like to apologize should there have been any omissions.

Key: *a* = above
b = below
l = left
r = right
ar = above right
al = above left
Ace 143*b*, 153 & 173*b* (Mauritius), 163*a* (Ian Copping), 165*a* (Chris Arthur)
Laura Ashley Ltd 172*a*
Sheila Blake/Flora Magazine 160*a*
Arranged by Brenda Evans, photographed by Howard Nutt 140
Floracolour 154*r*
Flower Council of Holland 126, 127, 129*a*, 132–3, 135*a*, 136*b*, 138–9, 145*a*, 147*b*, 150*b*, 153*l*, 156, 157*a*, 161, 162*b*, 164, 165*b*, 166*a*, 167, 168, 169, 170, 171*l* & *ar*, 173*b*
Image Bank 131*b* (Laurie Rubin), 142*a* (G. Obremski), 142*b* (Murray Accosser), 155*b* (D. Roundtree)
Arranged by Reverend Valerie Makin, photographed by John Searle 128*b*, 129*a*, 130*a*, 136*a*, 146*l*, 158
Arranged by Anne Moore, photographed by Huntingdonshire Regional College 154*l*
NAFAS Ltd 144*b*, 145*r*, 146*r*
Arranged by Pam Phillips, photographed by Huntingdonshire Regional College 143*a*
Rachael Phillips/Flora Magazine 134
Arranged by Susan Phillips, photographed by Derek King Scott 150*a*
Pictor 141, 147*a*, 152, 155*a*, 157*b*
Mary Jane Vaughan at Fast Flowers 137*a*, 162*a*, 163
Pamela Westland 67, 96*b*, 173
Westminster Flower Festival, photographed by Paul Forrester 134*b*, 135*b*
Arranged by N. Willes, photographed by Howard Nutt 144*a*
WinterFlora 130*b*, 131*a*, 137*b*, 151
Worshipful Company of Gardeners, courtesy of Longmans Ltd 171*br*

All other photographs are the copyright of Quarto Publishing Plc. Quarto would like to thank the National Association of Flower Arrangement Societies of Great Britain (NAFAS Ltd) and *Flora Magazine* for their kind help.

Quarto would also like to thank Dorothy Frame for the index.